Victims
on Both Ends
of the Gun

TINA SCHUSTER

and

THE TARIQ KHAMISA FOUNDATION

VICTIMS on Both Ends OF THE GUN

Tariq
Khamisa
FOUNDATION

2022

Victims on Both ends of the Gun

ISBN-13: 978-1-956503-61-6

Waterside Productions
2055 Oxford Ave
Cardiff, CA 92007
www.waterside.com

Contents

Preface

LIVIA IACOBELLI, SEVENTH GRADE STUDENT

January 21, 1995. Twenty one days after New Year's and the promises that came with it. Five, four, three, two, one. Many of us can hope for a new job, a new puppy, to lose weight or to restart. But Tariq Khamisa, age 20, never expected that less than a month into 1995, his life would end. Tariq, a young man from Seattle, was in San Diego to begin his life and attend San Diego State University.

A pizza deliveryman to make some extra cash, Tariq was called in for a final delivery even though his shift was over. He headed out to his delivery location without any hesitation. Why would he second guess it? It was like any other delivery. He arrived at the location in San Diego's University Heights neighborhood. When he reached the address in an apartment complex, he saw no activity. No lights, no sound, nothing. He wandered around for a while until a neighbor told him the address did not exist. He was leaving the complex when four young men confronted him. The youngest, a boy, told Tariq to hand over the pizza, but Tariq resisted. As Tariq moved towards his car, the oldest one in the group at age 18, gave the youngest boy a gun and told him to shoot if the pizza man refused to hand over the pizza. To them Tariq was nothing but an object they could play God with. The boy fired, striking Tariq in his back. He tried to breathe but his lung filled with blood. Tariq stopped breathing and died.

The boy who shot Tariq Khamisa was Tony Hicks, age 14. His parents were part of rival gangs, which led to a life of violence. That night, January 21, two lives were taken: Tariq's and Tony's. Tony was facing a murder charge a few weeks after a new California law had been enacted. This new law allowed people as young as 14 to be tried as adults. Tony, at age 14, entered the Juvenile Detention system. At age 16, he was sentenced to 25 years for the murder of Tariq Khamisa, the 20-year-old with a promising future.

Tariq's father, Azim, sees a victim on both ends of the gun. He reached out to Tony's grandfather, Ples, and the two of them started a journey together. This is the story of the victims, their families and their varied paths to forgiveness.

Tariq Khamisa   Tony Hicks

Dedication

WRITTEN BY AZIM KHAMISA, TARIQ'S FATHER, AND TASREEN KHAMISA, TARIQ'S SISTER

Tariq Khamisa is always in our hearts and prayers. He continues to guide us and his spirit lives on through the peacemaking work we do in his name at the Tariq Khamisa Foundation (TKF) which he inspired as the legacy of his too brief life. We created the foundation to fuel his soul's journey, and in return he continues to fuel our passion and drive to fight for justice, equity and inclusion by teaching and inspiring, empathy, compassion, forgiveness, and peace. We honor his legacy and will continue to fight the good fight in his name for the rest of our lives. We love you, Tariq, and miss you so very much.

MY PHILOSOPHY OF LIFE
(Written by Tariq in 1992 at age 18
for an assignment his senior year of high school.)

These are six of the aphorisms that I base my life on. It means a lot to me to follow these aphorisms, and I try my utmost to.

1) "Hang in there when the odds are against you." I feel that this quote has helped me a lot in all the things I do, especially

in school and in sports. In wrestling, this quote has helped me out a lot.

Especially when you're matched up against that really good wrestler who's pinned everyone. This quote lets you know to tough it out even though the odds aren't in your favor, and a lot of the times when you do this you do end up coming out ahead when you were sure you weren't going to succeed.

2) "Treat people the way you would want to be treated." This is very important to me. I feel you should treat everyone with respect, and in return you will be treated with it. I feel that you should be kind to people and, in general, treat them the way you know you would want to be treated.

3) "Give life your best effort." I feel this is so important to me because if you always give life your best effort, in your mind you'll never be a failure. If you always give your 110%, you know you're trying your hardest and that gives you a good feeling of satisfaction even if you don't always come out ahead.

4) "Use your time wisely." I feel time not spent doing useful things is time wasted. I live by this quote because I feel time is the most precious commodity known to man; because once it's gone, it's gone forever. Time is one thing you can never get back once it's gone, so you should always spend your time wisely.

5) "It is all right to be disappointed but a winner can never allow himself to be discouraged."

This quote allows you to face the trials and tribulations of life, and still be able to walk with your head up. Failure is unavoidable, but you have to be able to move on and getting discouraged won't help you at all!

6) "Living by giving." I feel it is much better to give than to receive. It makes you feel so good to be able to give things to people; not only material things, but also special things. Perhaps a warm smile to that person who's having a bad day or some good advice to a person with a problem. Giving is a wonderful thing and I urge all of you to try it. It doesn't take much and it will give you a wonderful feeling of satisfaction.

Tariq Khamisa
March 6, 1974 – January 21, 1995

Part One

Tony Hicks

A shy boy of 8, Tony was one of the youngest children living with his great-grandmother, Ethel, in Los Angeles. He was less shy around other kids in the neighborhood. They loved going to a nearby arcade to play video games together. Tony's family extended past just the house he lived in to his neighborhood and all of the people around him.

When Tony's cousin Quincy was killed in a drive-by shooting, Tony's immediate response was to protect his family. Quincy was 14, six years older than Tony but not yet an adult. Since there wasn't a huge age difference between Tony and Quincy, Tony felt connected to the cousins who had been the target of this shooting. His cousin Willie, also 14, had been in the car with Quincy along with two other teenagers. Bullets struck all four boys in the car, but Quincy was the only one who died.

After Willie left the hospital, Tony felt particularly protective of him. He followed Willie around wherever he went so he could keep an eye on what he was doing. The shooting didn't deter Willie, and

1

Tony Hicks as a young boy

he continued living life as part of one of the most powerful gangs in LA. And Tony was his self-appointed protector. Despite the age difference, Willie had always gone out of his way to make time for Tony. They both lived in Tony's great-grandmother's house, and there was often an influx of family, sometimes up to 15 people, who shared the three-bedroom home.

Ethel's house was filled with laughter. There were always plenty of snacks and juice boxes. A rope swing hung from an enormous old tree in the backyard. At one point there was even a trampoline in the back, and Tony took pride in being able to jump higher than anyone else. The older kids would promise to catch the younger ones, but when they let them land on their own one too many times, Ethel decided to get rid of the trampoline.

When they weren't playing in the backyard, Tony's favorite afternoons came when Willie would buy him a treat from the ice cream truck that drove through the neighborhood. His cousin always had money to spend on Tony, and if it wasn't ice cream, he would sneak him sodas or candy. Sometimes they just watched cartoons together. Willie's favorites were Woody Woodpecker and Inspector Gadget. Tony loved spending time with Willie, and there was a sense of security knowing that the two boys were there for each other.

At Tony's great-grandmother's house, discussion about gangs had always been age appropriate. This meant that Tony never heard anything about older kids in their family being part of a gang. Tony learned about Willie's involvement in a gang from other kids talking about it at school. In Tony's world, he knew that Quincy and Willie had been shot in a vicious attack, but no one could explain to him *why*. Tony didn't understand yet what a rival gang was or how drive-bys were used for intimidation or execution. He didn't understand that Willie was a small piece in a much larger web of gang conflict.

Tony's mother's only concern was that Tony was safe. She knew the high-risk gang lifestyles of her uncles. As everyone saw violence increasing, Tony's mom told him that she had made arrangements for him to go live with his grandfather in San Diego. Although San Diego was only two hours away, his mother felt like it would create enough distance and provide a much more secure environment for Tony, then 9. She wouldn't be coming with him, which was the hardest part for Tony to understand. His mother had given birth to him when she was 14, and they grew up together. She was not just his mother, he saw her as his close friend as well. She planned to visit as often as possible, but because of her job she couldn't move with him. To please his mother, Tony appeared receptive to the idea of striking out in a new city. In reality, Tony had been working hard on numbing himself to self-protect. From what he knew of his grandfather, Ples Felix, Tony would have to learn an entirely new way of life.

Tony knew that Ples lived a very disciplined life. Ples had been a teenage father and was 16 when Tony's mother was born. As a result of becoming a father at a young age, Ples didn't have as many options to be able to support his family financially. One option available to him was to join the Army. He did this as soon as he could, and he was quickly promoted to become part of the elite Green Berets, serving two full tours in the Vietnam War. With a background like this, Tony understood why his grandfather had much stricter rules than in his great-grandmother's house in Los Angeles. When Ples and Tony met to discuss the move, Tony wanted to know how his life might change.

"Are you going to let me eat ice cream?" Tony asked. Ples explained that Tony wouldn't have unlimited ice cream, but that yes, he could still eat ice cream.

However, in addition to the new rules, Tony was worried about moving to a place where he knew no one. He had learned, though, that if he was quick to smile, the people around him thought he was fine. They wouldn't ask him too many questions. This had protected him well in Los Angeles. He really did want to make his grandfather and his mother happy, though, so when his mother decided to stay in Los Angeles and send Tony to San Diego, he smiled and tried to make the best of it.

When Tony transferred into a new elementary school in San Diego, he was enthusiastic at first. The new kids were curious about him, and he quickly made a couple of friends. Tony brought his enthusiasm for school home to his grandfather, and Ples could see it on his face. After the first few weeks, however, the smiles that Tony wore home didn't match the reports his teacher was sending home. The teacher said Tony was not doing his work. The teacher was concerned about Tony's classroom behavior. She said that when Tony ran into any kind of challenge, he would shut down instead of trying to work through

4

it. There were even times when the class was in the middle of working on an assignment and Tony would just stop and refuse to continue. The teachers began to see this behavior as defiant.

Ples could see that this behavior aligned with times when Tony was quieter at home. Some days, Tony made his anger and sadness clear. However, since Ples possessed a background in the military, he scrutinized Tony's life through a different lens. He saw most situations in life as missions. A person's experiences were either successful missions or mission failures. As a result, he often didn't see the gray area in between success and failure. Ples listened to the teacher and saw what was happening at school with Tony as a mission failure. He and his grandson spent many days trying to talk through why Tony wasn't taking part fully in school. One evening, the conversation between Ples and Tony quickly came to a head. Ples had made vegetarian lasagna, and they were eating an early dinner after school. Ples tried to cook healthy meals most of the time, and he introduced Tony to a mostly vegetarian lifestyle. Tony poked at the lettuce in his salad with a fork, but did not dig into the meal as he usually would.

Ples started in on the line of questioning he had been using for weeks. His tone wasn't angry. But the tone was forceful, implying that he wasn't going to let Tony sit quietly and avoid answering.

"Why aren't you doing the work that your teachers are assigning? You are aware of the fourth grade requirements, aren't you?"

Tony continued to push his food around on his plate, and he slid a green pepper slice from the lasagna into his mouth.

"Yes," he responded and offered nothing else.

"Then why aren't you doing your work?"

Tony put his fork down and looked up at his grandfather with a hurt look of betrayal. Some days Tony tried to defend himself, but on this day he looked resigned instead. His grandfather could read

5

his thoughts through his expression. *Why should I even try to defend myself? You're not on my side. You're on the teacher's side.*

Ples knew not to press the issue, but he also wanted to find a way for Tony to accomplish his mission at school. Tony's look made his grandfather reexamine his stance, and he decided he needed to figure out how to get on the same side as Tony.

He paused and chose his words carefully. "Is there anything I can do to help make this situation better with your teacher?"

Tony released the tension in his face and his eyes softened. "You can talk with my teacher about why she thinks I should be like everybody else."

His teacher didn't know Tony or what Tony was up against, but his grandfather realized that he could help reshape this relationship for him in school. Without intending it, Tony had just given his grandfather a new and clear mission.

"OK, son. I'll go, and I will set up a conference with the teacher. I think it's important that you be really clearly understood and that you understand that you have a voice in the school. I want you to know you have a voice with your teacher."

Tony relaxed and began to work through his lasagna with enthusiasm.

The next day, Ples started on his new mission. After dropping Tony at his classroom door, he stopped by the principal's office and said he would be seeking a conference with Tony's teacher within the next few days. Once the date was set with the teacher, Ples went home content to plan for his mission.

A few days passed, and on the day of the meeting, the whole group gathered in the classroom. Tony, his grandfather, the teacher and the principal sat surrounded by the empty desks.

Tony's grandfather thanked everyone for agreeing to meet, and then he began with some of his points. Since he had met with Tony the previous day to prepare for the meeting, he had thought about how he wanted to lead into the conversation. His goal was to leave the meeting with Tony feeling like he had a voice in the classroom. One of the bigger things that Ples learned from Tony was that, as the new kid, he felt ignored. His classmates knew each other, and Tony didn't feel like he had a place with them. If they left the meeting with Tony feeling a sense of belonging in the classroom, Ples would consider the mission accomplished.

"Tony isn't a student that requires special treatment. But he does require inclusionary treatment."

The teacher crossed her arms and slightly leaned back into her chair. "I have tried to include Tony, but he is a sullen child." She was directing most of her responses to the principal with an occasional glance toward Ples.

"He isn't clear in his speaking, either," she continued. "He mumbles."

Ples turned to Tony, sitting next to him. "You mumble?"

Tony responded immediately. "I never mumble." He looked directly at his grandfather when he answered.

"It seems we have a conflict here," Tony's grandfather said looking back and forth calmly between the teacher and Tony. "You say he mumbles. He says he never mumbles. This could be a perception problem for either person."

The principal was taking notes and didn't interrupt.

Tony's grandfather continued. "From this point on, when he speaks to you, you will hear him clearly." He looked at Tony next. "Is that right? Will you speak clearly?"

"Yeah, I will speak very clearly," Tony looked at the teacher for the first time.

The principal finished writing his notes and looked up still holding his pen. "It seems like we are on our way to a plan." He turned to a blank

Tony Hicks with his mother and grandfather Ples Felix

page in his notepad and began writing while talking. "Anytime Tony's teacher is experiencing any kind of challenges with Tony, she will send a note home with Tony. If he isn't doing his homework or if he isn't complying with the rules of the classroom, a note will go home."

The teacher nodded, and the principal continued. "Tony's grandfather will receive the note and go over the challenge at home with Tony, and he will make notations to send back to school with Tony. If either of you need any additional followup, you can discuss on the phone or we can schedule another meeting."

The group continued to work out some of the more minor details of the plan, and everyone left the meeting feeling satisfied. The principal had the impression that Tony wasn't the only new student in the school experiencing some kind of disconnect, and he explained that he hoped this plan could serve as a model for other students and their families if they were feeling this way.

Life in school improved for Tony, and when he hit a rough spot again academically the next year, he didn't keep it to himself. His fifth grade teacher was concerned and arranged a plan for Tony to stay after school to work with teachers and with Ples at home to catch up with the rest of the class. In the middle of that school year, he had been on the verge of having to repeat the grade. After working with his teacher and grandfather, he had passing grades by the end of the semester. He entered sixth grade with his class and was able to move into middle school with an academic win under his belt.

This experience of falling behind and struggling, but then asking for help, was one of Tony's biggest achievements. He felt so empowered when he entered middle school that he often returned to his elementary school to work with students in similar situations. The elementary teachers had arranged for Tony to tutor students struggling with reading. By sharing his story, he let those students know that by accepting support, they could also turn things around. The teachers loved having Tony return as an example and inspiration for the other elementary students.

During sixth grade, on a visit to his mother in Los Angeles, Tony had an experience that brought his anger and confusion to the surface again. His cousin Willie, who was now 17, was killed in another drive-by shooting. Tony wasn't there when it happened, and he blamed himself for not being able to prevent it. Willie was washing his car in the morning in front of Great-Grandmother Ethel's house. Tony was across town at another relative's house. He had been uncooperative all morning. His mother told him they were going to Grandma Ethel's house, but he didn't want to go. He knew that meant his mother would leave him there for the whole day, and he really wanted to spend time with her. By the time he agreed to go to his great-grandmother's, he was sulking and upset that his mother was not going to spend the day with him. As soon as they turned onto Grandma Ethel's street, they saw one of his mom's friends walking toward them. Her friend didn't make eye contact with Tony. He whispered to his mom: "Willie is dead."

As Tony and his mother approached the house, there were not yet emergency vehicles on the scene. However, a few people were standing near the car and Willie's body. Tony could see holes in the car and windshield of the brown Cadillac. On the other side, the passenger door was open, and Willie's feet were sticking out. It was obvious that he had been washing his car and tried to dive into the car to avoid the bullets. Wille's white and red high-top sneakers were a lifeless pop of color etched in Tony's gray memory.

Anger and guilt consumed Tony. He felt like Willie's death was his fault. If he hadn't taken so long to agree to go to his grandmother's, maybe he would have been there in time to save him. Willie was the cousin Tony was supposed to protect since the shooting years earlier. Other thoughts crossed his mind. If he had arrived on time, maybe Tony could have died in Willie's place, which would have at least given his life some purpose.

Willie's funeral was similar to others he had attended for his cousins. Willie's family — and his extended family of gang members — were there. These gang members flooded the funeral with a sea of red. They filed by the closed casket, placing red bandanas onto the growing mountain on top.

After Willie's murder, Tony returned to San Diego and felt completely powerless. He no longer cared about school, and instead he went through the motions of attending. By seventh grade, Tony had stopped tutoring at the elementary school, and he found a group of friends who seemed to focus only on having fun and living in the present moment. They never talked about the past or what they hoped for in the future. Tony only wanted to do things that would keep him numb and push away the bad feelings.

Before Willie's death, Tony worked hard to push his anger aside so he wouldn't disappoint his mother or grandfather. But Tony's grandfather saw the anger surface again. Ples saw it when Tony stopped doing his homework and his grades dropped. Tony started smoking weed to fog his thinking and dull his emotions. They got to the point where Tony and Ples were talking almost every night about what was going on at school. Tony let his grandfather know that he was mad, but he couldn't really say who he was mad at. Ples knew that Tony was angry at many different people and things that had happened in the world.

Tony had a big hole in his heart from growing up with a stranger for a father. He had seen his father only three times up until that point, and all three times his father essentially ignored him. His father was a teenager when Tony was born, and he never gave support to Tony's mom. Since Tony's father had been the only boy in his house, he was expected to take care of his sisters and mom. He wasn't mature enough to deal with a child of his own. He was an older teenager who didn't want to be bothered with a little kid. On the other hand, Tony's mom thought of Tony as her baby no matter how old he was. The two had a special connection. Once, Tony asked his grandfather, "How do you think my mom's doing?" A few seconds later the phone rang. This connectedness made living apart hard. Tony struggled with her decision in his heart, although it made sense to him in his head. He experienced his mother's love consistently and then this mother's love was suddenly gone. And now he was angry and confused about his cousin's death. By seventh grade, when Tony was 12, he had become very angry.

Ples hoped that therapy would help Tony sort out his feelings and focus on school again. Seeing a therapist was not part of their culture, but Ples decided to enroll him anyway — intentionally with an African-American male psychologist who might be able to relate to Tony's anger. If Tony could talk about his feelings with a neutral person, like a therapist, Ples was sure this would be healthy for him. He had waited until Tony's anger was overruling his ability to focus on school or be productive in any part of his day. Instead Tony would become lost in his Sega video games or go to friends' houses with similar family dynamics. It made Tony feel normal when he went to his friend Henry's house and saw that Henry had no father in his life, either. He had an older brother and a mother who worked long hours to support the family. The teenagers in the house spent almost all of their time unsupervised.

By eighth grade Tony had been attending therapy for almost a year, but his grades weren't improving and his anger was always right below the surface. His grandfather was noticing a pattern of a few good days for Tony when he would be happy and finishing his work at school. Then he would slump quickly into consecutive low days. One Friday at breakfast, after his grandfather had made him a vegetarian omelette, grits and toast, Tony's favorite breakfast, he asked Tony, "How are you doing?"

He knew Tony wasn't feeling enthusiastic about his day, and Ples hoped he might offer some information to help Tony navigate his day at school.

"I want you to do all you can to focus your mind on having a good day at school today. Have fun and play."

Tony responded, "OK, Daddy." Tony called Ples Daddy ever since he had moved in.

His grandfather had an orange and an apple on the table, and he offered both to Tony. Absently, Tony took the apple and put it in his backpack.

By the time he returned home Friday evening, Tony's spirit had fallen even further. He hadn't done his work all week so he knew a note was coming for Ples.

Ples read the note and asked, "How are things going at school?"

"Not too good," Tony responded. "Things are bad at school." He handed his grandfather the weekly handwritten note from his teacher. The list wasn't long, but there were three assignments that Tony hadn't done that he'd have to complete by Monday.

Instead of addressing it right away, Ples said they would talk after dinner. He could sense that Tony was upset. Ples offered, "Why don't you watch some TV while I make dinner?"

Ples thought about how to approach the conversation while he sliced the vegetables for his pasta sauce and prepared the garlic bread. Ples knew that when Tony was upset he wouldn't talk much. Since Tony had blown off three assignments, he knew Ples was going to find out about them, and that explained his lack of motivation to go to school that morning.

As predicted, Tony didn't talk at dinner, but they both finished their pasta before starting the conversation. After they cleaned their plates, Ples told Tony he wanted to have a chat with him. Tony knew what that meant. They both headed to Ples' bedroom, where he had a comfortable space on the floor for them to conference. The floor was carpeted and Tony usually grabbed the same large brown and beige striped pillow to sit on while Ples sat directly on the carpet. They both leaned their backs against the platform bed for support.

Ples knew if he asked *why* Tony wasn't doing his work, Tony would get upset and possibly defensive. Instead, he decided to try to help Tony recognize that he needed his grandfather's assistance. This way they could set up a plan together.

Tony Hicks with his great grandmother Nicola Hall Felix and
grandfather Ples Felix

Ples started. "It seems like you have been having some bad days. I'm looking at the notes your teachers are sending home, and they say you aren't doing all your work."

Tony didn't respond right away. He inhaled slowly and paused before speaking. "I'm tired of this school, and I'm tired of these people."

When Tony took this path of reasoning in the past, his grandfather tried to help him see choices he might have instead of feeling like things were out of his control.

"What do you think should be available to you as a choice other than where you are now by going to school?"

"I don't know," Tony responded quietly, looking at his food.

"What do you think could be a choice for you to interact with people other than the people you interact with?"

"I don't know."

Ples softened his voice. "Help me understand what you do know. I understand what you don't know. What is it you are feeling that you want to share?"

Instead of responding, Tony's face darkened and his grandfather could see the frustration and anger starting to fill his face.

Ples kept his calm tone and continued, but he understood how angry Tony was inside. He was worried how that anger might turn into action.

"Look. It's very important that you understand what I'm about to tell you." He waited to let this sink in. Tony looked up as his grandfather continued. "Sometime real soon, someone is going to give you a loaded handgun and tell you to shoot somebody. What are you going to do?"

Tony held his gaze. "Daddy, I would never do that."

"That's what you tell me. You're looking me in my face, and that's what you tell me. But what are you going to tell that fool out there who gives you a gun and tells you to shoot somebody? Do you have the strength to tell him no?"

Tony straightened himself in the chair and repeated, "I wouldn't do that."

Ples let the answer suffice and moved past it. "Tell me about your tomorrow. You only had a few assignments this week so I'll make a deal with you. You do the missing assignments, and you do your home chores. Once you get that done, you're free for the rest of the day. You can go to the park and be with your friends and go play. But you got to do those things first. Can you do that?"

Tony agreed, and the air in the room felt a little lighter after they came to an agreement, together.

The next morning, Ples left to start his Saturday errands. Usually he went grocery shopping for their planned meals for the week and did laundry or anything else that took more time than Ples had during the week to get accomplished. As they agreed, Tony was left at home in the morning to work on his missing school assignments and his normal weekend chores. Hoping to be home by midday to check in with his grandson, Ples sped through his Saturday activities.

When he returned home, Ples walked in and noticed the air was still and the house was dark. There was no sign of movement. While running errands, Ples had calculated how long it would take for Tony to complete his assignments and house chores, and he knew there was no way Tony could have already finished. Ples had a sinking feeling in his stomach as he began to look around the house. On his own bed, Ples found a note. It simply read:

Daddy- I've run away.
Love, Tony

His sinking feeling had been confirmed. He looked around and found some items were missing. Tony had emptied the bowl of loose coins near the door, and he had taken his Sega system and games. However, the most concerning missing item was a pump shotgun that Tony's grandfather had hidden in the house. The shotgun was always secured and locked away. At this point, Ples' sinking feeling had turned into genuine concern. Tony had a weapon.

Ples grew up in Los Angeles, and he didn't have a positive relationship with the police. When he was in middle school, the police were oppressors in his neighborhood. He recalled times when he would be hanging out with his friends and police officers would push Ples or his friends against a wall and threaten them that they were being watched, even if they were doing nothing wrong. In spite of that memory and the lack of positive relationship with the police,

Ples knew that Tony had run away. Thinking only of Tony's safety, he called the police and filed a report for his missing grandson.

Immediately after hanging up, Ples called his daughter to let her know her son had run away. She suggested that Ples call his friend, who was a pastor, to seek advice. Ples could be impulsive, and his instinct was to go to Henry's or Sam's house until he found Tony and could drag him home. Henry and Sam were Tony's best friends, and he was almost certain he would find him there. However, Ples' pastor friend advised otherwise, talking him through the scenario.

"If you go out and find him in the presence of other kids, you know Tony isn't going to be compliant. And you aren't going to take that well. Ples, I know you well enough to know that someone is going to get hurt if you go out and find Tony."

Ples knew the pastor was right, and he decided it would be better for everyone if Ples stayed home.

Meanwhile, Tony knew he shouldn't have run away, but he woke up that Saturday morning angry at everyone, and he wanted to get away from his grandfather's rules. The conversation the night before had led to a temporary reprieve from his grandfather's scrutiny, but he knew that wasn't going to last. He had no desire to work on his missing assignments, and definitely wasn't interested in completing his chores at home.

The previous few weeks had moved really quickly for Tony, as he was starting to get involved with a neighborhood gang. Ples didn't know about that part of his life. Tony had come to realize that gangs offered people in his neighborhood a sense of belonging. This makeshift model of protection and family often imitated behavior that Tony and his friends had seen on TV. It used to be that if you wanted to demonstrate commitment to the gang, you had to be "jumped in" to see if you could take a good beating. Tony had heard of some people driving down the street and shooting someone or taking part in other types of destructive behavior to justify their membership to the gang. Most of the pressure for this kind of activity came from the expectations the boys put on themselves. It was understood that extreme efforts to join showed commitment to the gang, putting them closer to the center of power.

Henry, Sam and Tony had known each other since fourth grade. As they began doing menial tasks for the gang, they adopted nicknames. Henry was "Hank," Sam was "Quick," and Tony was known as "Bone." They all answered to the leader, Joseph, known as "Jo Jo" in the gang. Tony had never hung around someone as angry and as violent as Jo Jo. Within the set, a term for the smaller group within the larger gang, members were both in awe of and afraid of Jo Jo. It was a highly dysfunctional group of mostly teens with varying views on what it meant to be a part of the gang.

When Tony met up with his friends that morning, they told him that Jo Jo had killed a homeless man the previous month because he said he wanted to simply "try out the gun." Some of the gang members who saw this happen became scared and left. There was one gang member, Paul, whose house had become an informal command center. They stored their marijuana and weapons there. After Tony told his friends that he had run away from home that morning, Henry and Sam brainstormed what they should do. Eventually they decided they should go to Paul's house and try to get Tony to earn more status in the gang. Living under his grandfather's strict curfew, Tony hadn't been able to participate in gang activities as much as Henry and Sam had. Tony knew that once Jo Jo accepted him into the group, he would need to go along with whatever Jo Jo asked of him.

By the time they got to Paul's house, other gang members were already partying. They all sat in Paul's room, and Sam and Henry announced to Jo Jo that Tony had run away from home.

"Maybe now you can make it to a meeting," Jo Jo responded, looking at Tony, while everyone in the room laughed.

Tony felt anger growing, but he didn't say anything.

Sam watched him and gave him an opening. "What are you going to do now?"

Tony responded immediately, "Go to LA."

As soon as Jo Jo heard this, he turned to the group and said, "If you aren't planning to go back there, we should hit your house."

A "hit" was a break-in, and this set was doing more of these burglaries. Although Tony still loved and feared his grandfather, he knew that Jo Jo was testing his commitment to the gang. He didn't want to be seen as weak.

Tony shrugged his shoulders and said, "I don't care."

Sam looked at Tony like he knew what he was feeling, but he said nothing.

Jo Jo, Sam, Henry and Tony started walking toward Tony's grandfather's house. Jo Jo asked Tony about valuables in the house. Tony's Sega game system was the only thing that he felt was of value to him. He knew his grandfather had guns, but he wasn't sure how many. When they reached the house, Henry and Tony were ordered to stay as lookouts in the alley. Sam and Jo Jo used Tony's key to let themselves in.

Tony was relieved when Sam and Jo Jo came out of the house. He was afraid his grandfather would come home before they could leave. Jo Jo carried a grocery bag with the Sega gaming system. Sam was walking stiffly because he had put Tony's grandfather's gun down the inside of his pant's leg.

Tony Hicks and Ples Felix

As the boys walked back to Paul's house, Jo Jo was upset that there was nothing of real value at Tony's house. This put more pressure on Tony to come through and impress Jo Jo in another way so the gang would accept him.

The boys made it back to Paul's house and spent the rest of the afternoon drinking and smoking weed. Girls came in and out of the house throughout the day to party, and the day stretched out into a foggy haze. Tony's unease about running away and breaking into his grandfather's house slowly faded. By 8:30 p.m. everyone in the house was hungry and started talking about jacking a pizza — ordering a pizza and taking it without paying. One of the girls in the group, Sandra, had a mature sounding voice although she was a teenager. After a little negotiation, she agreed to make the call and give a fake address in exchange for two slices of pizza.

First, the group discussed a few pizza place options before one girl suggested DiMille's. She knew the restaurant was nearby on Adams

Avenue. When they called, an employee said they would be able to add their order to the last delivery of the night. Sandra gave them the address on Louisiana Street, a few blocks from Jo Jo's house. Although the building address was correct, she told them it was for Apartment D. The building had no Apartment D.

Jo Jo was the mastermind behind the pizza jacking, and he made a plan to take Sam, Henry and Tony with him. Tony knew Jo Jo might accept him into the gang by the end of the night if he did what was asked of him. Because Jo Jo was 18, a legal adult, he didn't want all the responsibility for committing the pizza jacking. They figured that Tony and Jo Jo could hassle the deliveryman and Sam and Henry would take the pizzas. It wasn't the first time that Jo Jo had jacked a pizza with a group. The boys had been drinking all day, and it was easy to go along with Jo Jo's plan.

After ordering the pizza, the boys walked the few blocks to the address they called in. Sam started off carrying the gun they chose to take with them. Jo Jo had taken the 9 mm pistol in a burglary the previous day. They decided Sam would carry the gun in his hoodie pocket until they reached the apartments. Once there, Sam would hand Tony the gun, and Tony would hold the gun out. While he did this, the other three boys would rob the pizza man. Tony was confused about why he was the one holding the gun since he had a cast on his hand from an earlier injury. But he didn't ask any questions. He didn't want Jo Jo or the gang to reject him. They waited across the street from the building until the pizza man pulled up. Henry was jumpy and clearly uncomfortable. He separated from the group because he said it would look suspicious if they were all together. Sam and Jo Jo joked about how afraid Henry was, how he always acted this way on missions. Tony didn't want them to say the same thing about him, so he stayed with the group and joined in making fun of Henry's jumpiness.

21

After a few minutes, a car pulled up and the pizza man got out. With a look of relief, Sam handed the gun to Tony. It was Tony's first time holding a gun. It felt heavy and awkward in his hand.

The pizza man was in a hurry, taking the steps two at a time. The boys watched him enter the building and crossed the street to wait near his car. After a few moments, the pizza man came out of the building to check the address before going back inside. He moved quickly in his frustration. The three boys were looking to Jo Jo for guidance. He said that when the deliveryman came back out they would jack the pizzas. Soon, the boys watched the pizza man storm down the stairs back to his car.

As the pizza man threw the pizzas in the back seat, Tony stepped out in front of the group. He pointed the gun awkwardly with his left hand, the cast immobilizing his dominant right hand. He held the gun sideways, the way he had seen it done on television. Jo Jo was behind Tony and might have been visible as well, but Tony wasn't certain. The pizza man looked up, surprised. In Tony's mind, the pizza man was more surprised than afraid, and this made Tony angry because he felt like he wasn't being taken seriously.

"Give me the pizza," Tony said, still holding the gun.

"No," the pizza man said as he backed slowly toward the driver's door.

"Give me the pizza," Tony demanded again.

The pizza man mumbled something that wasn't clear to Tony. As he was mumbling, the pizza man got in the driver's seat and closed the door while never looking away from Tony. He began rolling up the window while still watching what was happening.

Tony was expecting some kind of shift in his expression, but nothing changed. Unsure how to deal with the defiant pizza man, Tony looked to Jo Jo for guidance.

Within seconds, Jo Jo yelled at Tony, "Bust him, Bone! Bust him!"

Time seemed to pause. Tony had felt as if he were in a fog all day, and Jo Jo's command to "bust him" took a moment to settle in. And then, after a few seconds, Tony fired one shot through the window. The pizza man stopped rolling up the window and slumped over the wheel. At this moment, Tony saw a spotlight fall on the two of them — a deliveryman who refused to give up his pizzas and a 14-year-old holding a gun. The light blocked out everything in the background and shone on only the two of them. Tony stood transfixed by this light. He could hear the pizza man gasping for air.

The spotlight started to fade out, and Tony became aware of the other boys' voices.

"Run, Bone!" They were all yelling at him to run.

"Don't drop the gun!" another yelled.

As they ran, none of the boys thought about the pizzas they had been trying to jack. None of the boys thought about the unpaid receipt in the pizza man's back pocket for $27.24. Instead, Tony and the boys just ran.

Part Two

Tariq Khamisa

SUMMER 1994

Packing for the trip to Kenya had been harder than Tariq thought it would be. Kenya, like most of East Africa, didn't really have distinct seasons; it was too close to the equator for that. However, it could be as warm as 80 in the day and then drop to freezing weather at night. The flight was going to be long, and he knew he would need to bring extra batteries for his Walkman so he could listen to cassette tapes of his favorite music. Tariq had every Bob Marley tape he could get his hands on, as well as tapes of other reggae bands. Listening to reggae would allow him to relax and spend time inside his own head. Although he had never been to Kenya, he had heard stories from his parents about how life was before they fled the country and moved to Vancouver. They left in the 1970s when dictator Idi Amin assumed power in neighboring Uganda. Amin threatened to take over Kenya, and his soldiers were killing Kenyans in Uganda. When their family decided to

Tariq Khamisa as a young boy

leave, Tasreen, Tariq's older sister who had been born in Kenya, was still in diapers. Tariq wasn't born yet. However, as he grew up away from Kenya, his parents built in him memories of this country through stories that he hadn't had a chance to experience in person. That is why when Tasreen graduated from the University of Washington, she asked for a trip to Kenya to visit her parents' homeland. Even though their parents were divorced when Tariq and Tasreen were younger, they still worked well together for the sake of their kids. Tariq and Tasreen's dad decided to grant her wish and pay for both of them, their mom, and their aunt to travel together for two whole months to visit family in Kenya.

Tariq's mom and aunt had planned most of the trip. They knew the area, as well as the extended family waiting to welcome them all back. He knew they were going to spend about two weeks in Nairobi, the capital of Kenya, and two weeks in the beach town of Mombasa, where his family still had some land. They also planned to go to Kisumu, on the other side of the country. It was on the water, too, but not the ocean. Kisumu lay on the east side of massive Lake Victoria, which was surrounded by neighboring Uganda and Tanzania.

Tariq finished packing enough jackets, pants and T-shirts to last at least a week before he would need to do laundry. Since he knew they would be doing a lot of walking, he packed his comfortable pair of beige Birkenstock sandals and his favorite pair of Doc Martens boots. His boots took up a lot of his suitcase, but he couldn't imagine two months without these heavy black shoes. Their weight grounded him.

Although he was excited at the prospect of traveling, he felt unsettled about leaving Jennifer, his girlfriend, for two months. They had built their worlds around each other. Tariq had always had back-to-back girlfriends starting in high school, and he never had trouble meeting girls. However, Jennifer was different. Once they were introduced at San Diego State University as freshmen, they became inseparable. When people were around them, they said they could feel the energy that connected Tariq and Jennifer. When Tariq's family met Jennifer, they told him that what they had was different from any of his previous relationships. Jennifer knew how important this trip was to him, so she encouraged him to go. They agreed to write letters and keep journals to read when Tariq returned to San Diego.

From the moment he boarded the plane, he started to miss Jennifer, and it was visible. From the seat next to Tariq, Tasreen noticed right away that he seemed distracted amid the excitement of their long flight. They were so close as siblings that there was no way he could hide it from her. As children, they had twin beds in the same shared bedroom. Before the divorce, when their parents were fighting all the time, Tariq and Tasreen knew they always had each other. Part of this closeness grew from their time in elementary school right after the divorce. Their mother was working to try to support her family, and the kids would go to after-school programs. However, other children often picked on them because of their darker skin. After some older boys attacked Tariq, first grade and Tasreen, third grade Tariq decided that instead of after-school care, they would walk home together, lock the door, and take care of themselves until their mom got home from work. While other kids were playing in the neighborhood, Tasreen and Tariq stayed in their house, playing with each other.

The trip to Kenya gave them a rare chance to spend time together since college had separated them. When they did see each other, Tasreen usually came to San Diego. During previous visits, she had hung out with Jennifer many times. The two women got along really well. Jennifer was kind-hearted and down-to-earth just like her brother, and Tasreen assumed that's why they worked so well together as a couple. Both Tasreen and Jennifer were sociology majors, and Jennifer shared with Tasreen that she wanted to work in one of the social services departments after college so she could give back to the community. Tasreen was also in a relationship, and she could relate to the way that Tariq was missing Jennifer while the siblings were gone in Kenya.

On their way to Kenya, the four travelers spent a couple of days in London, and Tariq took the lead on getting them around. He was fearless when it came to trying something new. They settled into their traveling roles fairly quickly. Tariq was the independent explorer. He dove right into figuring out the complicated London train system, and he embraced traveling in London with the same passion that he embraced everything new in his life. The entire time in a new city, he seemed at ease and comfortable, while the other three travelers were more reserved. They let him take the lead.

In London and throughout the entire two months spent abroad, Tariq and Tasreen shared a room again, like they had when they were kids. For both siblings, the time in Kenya was eye-opening. In Washington state, they had grown up in a community where they were very aware of their skin color. However, being in Kenya was the first time Tariq and Tasreen became aware of what inequity in society really looked like. Even though they both saw this inequity in Kenya, it hit Tariq harder in his soul. When they arrived in Mombasa, Tariq saw very quickly that Indians owned almost all the larger luxury homes and ran many of the businesses. His understanding of who had the power was completely turned on its head. Tariq and Tasreen's skin color had always made them feel like outsiders. In Kenya, they were no longer outside the power structure, but they were at the top of it looking down. When he saw black Kenyans hired as drivers or house cleaners, his face tightened. Although he had no part in setting up the power structure in Nairobi, Mombasa or Kisumu, seeing it bothered him.

Tariq befriended one of the local boys who worked in his relatives' house in Nairobi. When packing to move to their next travel location, Tariq gave his Walkman to the boy, Anasa, who had worked in the house cleaning up after them. Anasa, 12, helped his mother with some of the domestic work around the big house that Tariq's relatives owned. When Tariq gave him his Walkman, Anasa's face erupted in an incredulous smile. He turned the Walkman over, asking how music could come out of such a little machine.

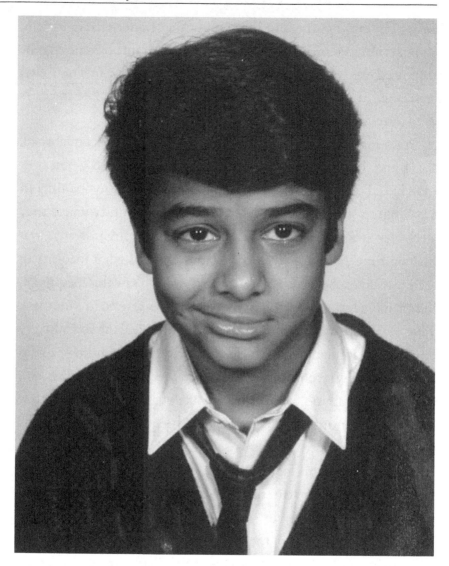

Tariq Khamisa school picture

Tasreen asked her brother as they pulled away, "How can you just give your stuff away? You love your Walkman."

Tariq felt lighter with no regret. "I can always buy another Walkman. Anasa can't."

In the seaside city of Mombasa, Tariq and Tasreen spent their days by the pool or on the beach, dining on meals prepared by a personal chef. They sat in comfortable silence or talked about what was important to them in life and love. One day, Tariq seemed troubled. After a little prodding, he said he felt torn up about his relationship with his dad. Everyone in the family knew that Tariq decided to leave Washington and go to school in San Diego in an effort to mend his relationship with his father.

"I just never felt that he valued what I valued," Tariq said. He turned and looked at Tasreen. "Do you remember how you came to every wrestling match of mine, and every football game?"

She nodded.

"I loved that you were there. But I just wish that he would have come, too."

"Dad?" she asked.

"Yeah. I tried to act like I didn't care when I was in high school. But I did, and it hurt."

"Do you think being in San Diego has made things better?" she asked.

Tariq thought about the question for a while before answering.

"I don't know if they are better. But I'm getting to know the real Azim Khamisa. I told him that when I moved to San Diego. I was tired of just hearing about the fake Azim Khamisa from him and everyone around him."

Tasreen didn't respond, but she nodded. They had talked about the fake and real Azim. Tariq considered the fake Azim to be the man who was a successful investment banker. He traveled all over the world as a consultant to companies that were trying to acquire other companies or sell their own. Working sometimes 100 hours a week, he would return home exhausted and uninvolved with the

31

people who should have been closest to him — his family. This was how Tariq had felt.

Tasreen, on the other hand, had always connected with her dad. She planned to go into business after college, and the two of them made sense to each other. Tariq wanted to be a photographer or a writer. When he talked about his dream job as a photographer for National Geographic, his father didn't see the value in becoming an artist. These misaligned expectations for Tariq's life strained their relationship. In the time they were growing up, the man was expected to provide, but that came with a cost: spending time with the family.

Tariq's relationship with his mom was the opposite. He would do anything for Almas, and that closeness remained even as Tariq got older. They protected each other. When Tariq was in middle school, he started wearing a necktie to school every day. One day, he came home from school deflated and told his mom that other kids were making fun of him. She first asked if he could stop wearing the ties to avoid ridicule. However, after hearing that he really liked dressing up to express himself, she helped support him with strategies to remain confident and also ignore the negative noise from other students.

Tasreen had a much more rocky relationship with their mother. Growing up, Almas was much more strict with Tasreen, but she would let Tariq get away with almost anything. Yet, Tasreen never resented Tariq for that. Instead, as an adult, she worked on the relationship with her mom, just like Tariq was working on his with his dad. They each felt like they had one parent who supported them, and Tariq and Tasreen always had each other.

When they left Kenya and returned to their individual lives, Tariq felt more clear on the direction he wanted to take his life. He brought it up with Tasreen in a conversation soon after she was hired at a corporation and felt like her life was on a good path.

32

Tariq told her he felt ready to leave San Diego and move back to Washington. Although he wasn't finished with college yet, this idea made Tasreen ecstatic. She had picked up on hints that both Tariq and Jennifer felt ready for a change. San Diego didn't fit Tariq like it fit his father, and Jennifer felt the same way about the city. They both valued an arts culture, and Tariq hadn't found the diversity he was looking for.

"I can't go until I save up at least a few thousand dollars, though," he said.

"If it's just a money thing, I can lend you the money." With her new job, Tasreen knew she would be making enough to lend to her brother the money it would cost to move back to Washington.

"No, I'm going to save up on my own. You know, I'm going to get a job first. I want to do this on my own."

Tasreen felt that she didn't need to press the issue. Tariq had always been independent, and Tasreen knew that he followed through when he had a plan. He was the most determined person she knew.

Tariq was true to his word. He found a job at a family-owned restaurant, DiMille's, delivering pizzas. DiMille's was in an area of San Diego called North Park, a 10-minute drive from Tariq's apartment in the neighboring area of Hillcrest. He loved the freedom of driving around the city, unlike other part-time office jobs his father had set up for him that he had promptly quit. Tariq was miserable in a desk job and found that although it distanced him further from his father, he couldn't be happy in the business world. He had returned from Kenya more determined than ever to find fulfillment in his life. In his words, it had destroyed his notion of an ideal life and turned it on its head. Although Jennifer hadn't gone on the trip, they both were inspired to redefine their place in the world — where and how they would live.

Tariq Khamisa in Kenya

A few months after returning from Kenya, Tasreen visited her boyfriend in San Diego. Soon after arriving, they got into an argument, and instead of the romantic weekend Tasreen envisioned, she left to spend the weekend with her brother. Tariq and Jennifer excitedly welcomed Tasreen to crash with them in their small Hillcrest apartment. The three of them turned the weekend into a time of deep conversations, good food and reminiscing about their trip to Kenya.

Jennifer had seen all the pictures, and Tariq had selected a few of his favorites to put together in a photo album for each family member who had made the trip. Photography was a passion of his, and sharing his craft was a way he showed his love. Tariq hadn't told Tasreen about her photo album yet, which he planned to send in a month after putting on all the finishing touches. But as they looked at pictures together, he watched her reaction to see which ones she connected with.

"Did this trip make a huge impact on you like it did for Tariq?" Jennifer asked Tasreen.

Tariq smiled and looked at Jennifer with a knowing recognition that she understood him.

"I would say it made an impact while I was there. I don't know if it changed much of my life when I got back here, though. Most things pretty much just returned to normal."

"I don't think they will ever be that kind of normal for me again after hearing all of the stories," Tariq said. "I still think about Haki."

Tasreen furrowed her brow, trying to remember who Haki was.

"You remember Haki? Our safari driver?"

Tasreen smiled. "Of course! There were so many new names, I just forgot for a second."

Tariq maintained his comforting hold on Jennifer's hand. "His story really is the one I can't stop thinking about. How he saw his family and neighbors being killed in front of him. And he left his own country of Rwanda and started an entirely new life. People like that are actual heroes that no one knows about."

Tasreen nodded as she recognized that same passion, frustration and energy that had bound Tariq in a space of wanting more from the world. At the end of their two days together, Tariq drove his sister to the airport. Instead of simply dropping her at the curb as usual, he chose to park in the short-term lot and walk inside with her. In airports at this time, a friend could accompany a passenger all the way to the gate. Tariq walked her to where she would board to return north, and he waited until the passengers lined up before he left. They hugged goodbye in a way that said "thank you" and

"I love you" all wrapped up in one embrace. Although she never liked arguments with her boyfriend, Tasreen was grateful for the time with her brother and Jennifer. She didn't know this was the last time she would see him.

After her visit to San Diego, Tasreen settled back quickly into her life, as did Tariq. He continued to work in between classes and time spent with his friends and Jennifer. Although much of his earnings went toward car insurance and his social life, he was able to save a little bit of each paycheck toward leaving San Diego. He worked many weekend shifts, since that was usually when the demand was highest and the tips were the best. Although DiMille's was located in the North Park neighborhood, they would deliver as far as 15 minutes in any direction. All the neighborhoods surrounding North Park were pretty densely populated.

January was especially busy for pizza delivery. With nighttime temperatures in the 30s or 40s, many people wanted to stay inside and have dinner come to them. This particular Saturday night in January was no exception. He wasn't supposed to work, but DiMille's had asked if Tariq would pick up the extra shift, and he needed the money. Tariq had taken back-to-back deliveries, and it seemed like he only had time to run into DiMille's to pick up an order and then run back out to deliver while the food was still hot. One of his orders was for an address close to his own in Hillcrest. He was able to grab Jennifer's favorite soda, Dr Pepper, deliver it to her at home, give her a kiss and tell her he loved her before heading back out for the final call of the night.

This final call was for an address close by in North Park on Louisiana Avenue. He knew the area well enough to know that this would lead to an apartment building nestled between other apartment buildings on the block. When he pulled up to the building, he turned on his hazard lights so he could run into the building without having to find a parking space. He pulled halfway into a driveway behind another car, but he often did this since he was usually in and out within a few minutes. Reaching into the back seat, he slid the pizza onto the flat of his arm. He ran up the stairs and started looking for Apartment D. Although all of the doors were labeled with numbers, he was having trouble finding the letter D for the address he was given. His car was still sitting with its hazard lights flashing, so he picked up the pace and figured the easiest thing would be to knock on a door and ask someone where the apartment was located. He knocked on several doors before someone answered. An older woman peeked through her cracked door to tell him there was no Apartment D in the building.

Worried about his car blocking the driveway, he decided he couldn't waste anymore time. It was rare, but sometimes he was given the wrong address. Tariq was ready for his shift to be over, so he decided that instead of wasting more time looking for an address that might not exist, he would head back to DiMille's and call it a night. He knew Jennifer hadn't gone out, and it was early enough that they could still watch a movie and have a night in.

Tariq tossed the pizza in the back seat, closed the door and reached the front door handle. That's when he noticed a group of boys step out of the shadows to approach him. They looked like kids, definitely not Tariq's age, and he fleetingly wondered if they had a parent around that he didn't see. He turned away from the boys and moved toward the front seat.

"Pizza man," Tariq heard one of the boys say. "Give me the pizzas."

Tariq noticed that the body of the boy who spoke was tense. Once Tariq turned to fully face the group, thoughts started racing through his head. How old were these boys? If the four of them caught up to him, would they take the pizza anyway? What right did these kids have to take a pizza and not pay? Then he saw the gun.

37

Tariq made a quick decision and jumped into the driver's seat, rolled up his window and started to back out. He could hear the boys yelling at each other.

He felt a powerful punch in his back, like he had been hit with a bat. When he looked to his left, there was nobody close enough to have reached him, although the boy with the gun looked frozen in place with the gun down by his side. Tariq locked eyes with the boy and then he was overtaken by an intense burning, worse than anything he had ever felt before.

"No, no, no," he started to repeat. He inhaled quickly to combat the feeling, but he couldn't get a full breath. He felt like he was inhaling water. Everytime he inhaled, he gasped for more air, but was met with a gurgling sound and only a trickle of air.

"Help me," Tariq murmured.

He closed his eyes to concentrate on breathing. Then the world went dark.

Tariq Khamisa writing in his journal

Part Three

The In-Between

Ples heard about the murder of a pizza deliveryman on the news, and he immediately had a bad feeling. He called his daughter and asked her to get a phone number from Tony if he called. Soon after they hung up, Tony called to tell her he had run away. He said he wanted to come to her in Los Angeles. As she had promised Ples, she told Tony she would call him right back and asked for a phone number. With the phone number, Ples knew that someone would answer the landline phone when he called. It was going to be up to Ples to determine which of Tony's friends answered so he would know where he could find Tony.

When Ples called, Henry answered, and Ples hung up. He recognized Henry's voice, but it was too late to act on the new information that night, so Ples decided to get up early the next morning to surprise Tony at Henry's apartment. He parked across the street and went to a pay phone at the corner store to call the police to let them know where his runaway grandson was staying.

Soon, Ples watched as two police cars pulled up. From across the street, he heard the officers knock on the door and ask for Tony

39

Hicks. Tony stepped outside, and the officers put him in the car. One officer crossed the street and told Ples he could pick Tony up at the station later. Ples felt relieved that Tony was secured, and he thanked the officer and let him know that he would pick him up later on after work. Ples figured that the two of them would have a long talk about his decision to run away.

Ples felt relief as the day passed until the phone rang. It was the police.

"Hello, my name is Detective Lambert."

Ples responded with a simple "Hello."

"I'm a homicide detective, and I need to report to you that we have your grandson in custody for the murder of a pizza deliveryman that took place in North Park this past weekend."

That unsettled feeling rose up again in Ples more clearly this time. He responded with a clear, "Thank you very much. I need to call my daughter."

"Your grandson is going to need an attorney."

Politely, but succinctly, Ples responded again, "Thank you. I'll call my daughter right now."

Ples made the heartbreaking call. He told his daughter the news and said he would find an attorney. They both knew there was nothing else they could do.

In the early 1990s, the crimes committed by young people almost doubled in the United States. San Diego and Southern California were part of this statistic. Starting in 1995, a new California law stated that juveniles as young as 14 could be tried as adults for certain crimes. The issue divided people in

San Diego. Some said people that young could be rehabilitated, and that they shouldn't be tried as adults because they weren't making adult decisions. The other side said some crimes, no matter the age of the perpetrator, should have adult consequences. The district attorney at the time, Paul Pfingst, had been tough on juvenile crime when he was running for office. He felt that people who killed in the course of a robbery should go to adult court. The policy wasn't automatic, however. The minors had to go through a hearing where the court would decide if minors were fit for the juvenile system or if they should be tried as adults.

When an anonymous informant called the hotline set up after Tariq's shooting, she told the police all the boys' names. The defense attorneys filed a challenge that the three minors should be tried as juveniles, not adults. The judge ruled that Henry and Sam would be tried as juveniles. However, because Tony had pulled the trigger, he became the first juvenile in the state to be tried as an adult. He was 14 years and 3 months old. On May 4, 1995, adult criminal charges were confirmed against Tony, and he was sent to an adult court.

———

The next week was a blur for Tariq's family. Kit, the wife of Azim's best friend, Dan, was able to set up the memorial service. It took place on a rainy Tuesday night with 250 people in attendance. Tasreen and Jennifer wrote messages, but neither had the strength to read them out loud. In Tasreen's letter, read by a friend, she said, "I feel so fortunate and blessed to have been his sister. There are no words

Ples Felix visiting teenage Tony Hicks in prison

to describe the feeling I have for him, and the pain I feel for our loss. My life will never be the same again."

Other friends and family read words from authors or spoke their own. A fellow San Diego State student who had attended the same mosque as Azim chanted Al-Fatiha, an Islamic prayer that honors the dead.

Jennifer's message, also read aloud by a friend, took some of Tariq's words from a recent journal entry: "Today I took control of my life. I can no longer blame others for my mistakes. I am responsible for my actions. No one is perfect — I don't want to be perfect. I know that I don't know. That's all I need to know." Jennifer reflected on these words in her spiritually optimistic message. "Although Tariq's body was young, his soul was very old. Somehow I know he made everything right in his life before he left us. Saturday night, January 21, 1995, was a good day for Tariq to die."

The day after the memorial service, Tariq's family flew to Vancouver to prepare for his funeral. In a proper burial in a mosque, there are no chairs or pews. All 1,400 people at the mosque sat together on the floor around Tariq's body, which was wrapped in a white shroud on the floor. At one point the entire mosque joined together in chanting the prayer for salvation as they each passed his body in a single-file line. This took 2½ hours, and the room was filled with a calming spiritual energy.

The energy continued as, according to tradition, the 500 men formed two lines facing each other as they passed Tariq's body toward the door. Eventually Tariq reached Azim, who helped place the body in the hearse.

At the gravesite and according to ritual, Azim jumped into the muddy grave and men passed his son's body down to him. He laid the body down and gently lowered Tariq's head as the last part of him to touch the earth. The men helped Azim from the grave, and each man walked by to place a shovelful of dirt.

When the judge confirmed that Tony would be tried as an adult, he began crying in the courtroom. His public defender had argued eloquently that Tony could be rehabilitated. He could change. The public defender pleaded on Tony's behalf. "He's only 14. ... We have seen how easy it is to damage a child and corrupt his spirit. We can convince him that he is unlovable and that he is responsible for his pathetic life. Lost in this fog of despair, this child is wounded and he is dying. ... You have a godlike power to determine whether these souls go down the road to salvation or damnation."

Azim Khamisa and Ples Felix holding the photos of Tariq Khamisa and Tony Hicks

The prosecutor, however, argued that Tony was a lost cause and that he had missed his chance to change or be rehabilitated. He said Tony had been given a chance to change when he moved in with his grandfather — in a loving and stable home with boundaries and discipline rooted in love. "With all the love, all the structure, all the discipline, [Tony] still ends up a gang member and a murderer," he argued. He said Tony had shown no signs of remorse in jail. With no proof that Tony had made any changes, the judge stood by his decision to try him as an adult.

Tony then began a legal journey that lasted a little more than a year and ended with his sentencing hearing. During that time some things changed with Tony. He spent a lot of time with Mike Reynolds, a San

Diego filmmaker and writer who worked with Tony to understand his story. During these meetings, Mike told Tony about the Tariq Khamisa Foundation, which had been started a several after Tariq was killed.

Azim created the Tariq Khamisa Foundation to use Tariq's death as a positive force. He hoped that by telling this story, Azim could find a way to protect other children. Five months after Tariq's death, Azim's supportive community had pulled together to start planning and finding resources to make the Tariq Khamisa Foundation a reality. Ten months after Tariq's death, TKF was officially launched. However, Azim felt that something was still needed to give TKF the best chance of achieving its mission. He asked the prosecutor if he could set up a meeting for Azim and Ples.

Azim and Ples met for the first time in the prosecutor's office. They shook hands, which started a bond between the two men that was cemented in their enduring commitment to the work of TKF. Azim told Ples that he didn't have any feelings of revenge toward anyone in Ples' family. Instead he acknowledged the grief that Ples also shared for Tony losing his life to a prison cell. Azim then told Ples about the work the Tariq Khamisa Foundation was planning to take on.

Ples responded with his sincere condolences for what had happened. He told Azim that their family was in his prayers and daily meditations. Without hesitation, Ples said he wanted to help the foundation in any way he could.

The meeting between these two men could have been cold and filled with hurt. Instead, the room felt warm and respectful. Neither man was tense. Instead, they were open with each other and the room filled with hope that they could work together to break the cycle of violence.

Mike Reynolds told Tony about the foundation, and Ples told Tony about it, too. They both told him that Azim did not seek revenge, but instead he offered Tony compassion and forgiveness. Tony could not believe this way of thinking at first. Eventually, after consistent updates about the work that was starting at TKF, Tony began to realize the consequences for what he had done. It's unclear the exact moment the change happened, but Tony began to think about what he had done in a different way. By the time he reached the sentencing hearing to give his plea, Tony had changed his plea from "not guilty" to "guilty." Tony felt remorse and emotional exhaustion. He decided that he didn't want to subject anyone's family to a trial. Instead, he pleaded guilty to murder in the first degree. His sentencing hearing was scheduled for three months after his plea.

On the day of the sentencing hearing, Judge Joan Weber of the San Diego Superior Court said, "I have been dreading this day. There is no pleasure in sentencing a boy to prison. I essentially see two lives destroyed by this."

Tony also spoke at the sentencing. He read his statement to everyone in the courtroom:

> *Good morning Judge,*
>
> *On January 21, 1995, I shot and killed Tariq Khamisa — a person I didn't even know and who didn't do anything wrong to me. On April 11, 1996, I pled guilty to first-degree murder because I am guilty. I wanted to save the Khamisa family and my family from further pain.*
>
> *From my grandfather, I have learned about the Khamisa family and their only son, Tariq. I have learned about the love they have for him. Through my grandfather and Mr. Reynolds, they have tried to explain to me the compassion the Khamisa family has for me.*

I have had a lot of problems in my life. Over the last year, while I have been in Juvenile Hall, I have thought about my problems. I wish I didn't have the type of life I had. I wish I had a relationship with my father. I think about the warmth that my grandfather gave me. I wonder why I didn't listen and learn. Now, I wish I would have listened to my grandfather.

At night, when I'm alone, I cry and beg God to let me out of here. I promise Him that I will be a better person. I won't mess up. When I see my mom, I want to hold her as tight as I can and beg her, 'Take me out of jail!'

However, I don't want to use my problems as an excuse for my actions. I think I would have gone to jail sometime, but I honestly don't think getting busted for a robbery or something like that would have changed me. I was too mad at everyone: my mom, my dad, my grandfather. When I first came to the Hall, I was mad at the district attorney and the people at the Hall for keeping me here. Now I'm just scared and mad at myself.

I'm alone at Juvenile Hall. Even though the people at the Hall are pretty cool, I'm still alone. I often think about the night I shot Tariq, especially when I'm alone in my cell. When it's dark and quiet, I wonder what it's like to die. I wonder why I'm still alive. Sometimes when I roll over in bed and I lay next to the cold wall, I feel as far away from everything as possible. I wonder if that's what dying feels like.

I still don't know why I shot Tariq. I didn't really want to hurt him or anyone else. I'm sorry for the pain that I caused for Tariq's father, Mr. Khamisa. I pray to God every day that Mr. Khamisa will forgive me for what I have done, and for as long as I live I will continue to pray to God to give him strength to deal with his loss.

> *My grandfather promised me that he will be Mr. Khamisa's friend and help him in any way he can for the rest of his life. I am very sorry for what I have done. Thank you for giving me the chance to speak.*

After everyone had spoken, the judge delivered her sentence. Tony was given 25 years to life in prison. She also announced that he would not be eligible for parole until he was 37 years old.

Part Four

Stories of Forgiveness

Azim

"When you choose forgiveness, the difficult emotions you've been holding onto will begin to fall away. When you are no longer holding onto those emotions that cause you pain and suffering, you will find that your heart once again has room for love and joy."
— Azim Khamisa

As a professional in domestic and international finance services, Tariq's father, Azim, traveled all over the world for work. In January 1995, he mixed business and pleasure and took a trip to Mexico. Although he had work to attend to while in Mexico, he also had been dating a Mexican woman, Mirtila, and he planned to spend a lot of his downtime with her. However, the pleasure side of the trip did not end as Azim hoped. Mirtila broke up with him. It wasn't completely unexpected for Azim, considering they had broken up three times before. Before Azim left the airport in Mexico, he arranged for his

51

Khamisa family picture:
Azim, his former wife Almas, daughter Tasreen and son Tariq Khamisa

best friend, Dan, and his wife, Kit, to pick him up at the airport in San Diego to get his mind off the end of his relationship. Kit and Dan were two of his closest friends and just the people to help distract him from the breakup.

As soon as Azim arrived in San Diego, Kit and Dan took him to a party. After the party, the group of friends returned to Azim's apartment to have a drink and catch up on everything that had happened in Mexico. By the time they all said goodnight, Tariq had already been killed. Yet, Azim went to bed unaware of the murder.

Azim woke up to let in his housekeeper who came twice a month. As she entered the house, she handed Azim a business card that had been left inside the screen door. When Azim read the name on the front of the card — Sergeant Lampert, San Diego Police, it didn't sound familiar. He flipped it over to see if there was any more information. Hand-written on the back of the card was a message: *We are trying to reach Tariq Khamisa's family.*

Azim was mildly curious but not overly concerned. He knew Tariq had a quick temper, and he thought he might have gotten into a fight. Azim would not have been surprised if Tariq had been arrested if things had gotten out of hand. He dialed the number and asked for Sergeant Lambert. The woman who answered the phone said the sergeant wasn't in the office. She hesitated for a moment and then delivered the message herself to Azim.

"I'm sorry. Tariq Khamisa was shot and killed last night."

Azim did not believe her. It might be a case of mistaken identity. He quickly called Tariq's home number fully expecting him to pick up. Of course he did not. Tariq's fiancée, Jennifer, answered, but she couldn't say anything through her sobbing. The homicide department had visited her home in the middle of the night and delivered the news.

This was when it hit. Azim's knees buckled and he collapsed to the floor, hitting his head against the refrigerator and curling up in a ball. He felt as though he couldn't stand to be in his own body. It was so devastatingly painful that he had his first out-of-body experience. As a practicing Sufi Muslim with a well established practice of daily meditaion, he belived he went into a loving embrace with God. He does not remember how long he was gone. It felt

53

like a nuclear bomb exploding in his heart, and when the explosion subsided, God returned him back to his body. As he was trying to process the details, Azim felt a pit in his stomach when he realized that he would need to call Almas and Tasreen and other members of his family to deliver the same shock.

The family was all in Vancouver since Azim's father had undergone open-heart surgery two days earlier. What should have been routine surgery took 12 hours. Some family went to Vancouver to be together as he recovered. Azim's and Almas' families had stayed close, even after the divorce, and Almas and Tasreen had traveled to Vancouver to support Azim's father and family.

With family spread out across Vancouver, Azim had to decide whom to call first. It had to be Tariq's mother, Almas. As soon as he heard her pick up, he blurted out, "Tariq has been shot. He is dead."

The only response he heard was a piercing shriek and the thud of the receiver hitting the floor.

Azim called his own mother next. He knew Tariq's sister, Tasreen, was staying with her. Azim's mother had the same response as Almas. From her screams, Tasreen assumed that something had happened to Azim's father after the surgery. Azim's mother was not able to communicate what had happened so Tasreen took the phone from her hand and heard the news from her father. Tasreen joined her grandmother in screaming in anguished disbelief.

Azim's last call was to Kit and Dan, his close friends in San Diego whom he had just seen the previous evening. He told the news one more time. In disbelief, they told Azim, "Don't do anything. We will be right over."

It took Kit and Dan 45 minutes to reach his house, but to Azim, it seemed like much longer. He spent the time pacing and fielding calls from his mother and his brother. As soon as Dan and Kit arrived, Azim and Dan stayed together in the townhouse while Kit drove to pick up Jennifer so they could all be together. When the two women returned, Dan and Azim were sitting together on the couch, and Jennifer and Kit sat on an adjacent couch. Jennifer told everyone what the police told her — witnesses saw four teenagers running from the shooting, but police hadn't found them yet. Dan, a frequent meditator and normally very grounded in Eastern philosophies that promoted love and peace, grew increasingly angry as Jennifer spoke.

Dan looked directly at Azim and spit out, "I hope they catch the little bastards and fry them."

Azim was surprised to realize he wasn't feeling vengeance in the same way as Dan.

"I see victims on both ends of the gun," he said.

Dan broke down and started crying. He asked his friend, "Where do you get this strength? If someone had taken my son's life, I would want the killer and his whole clan brought to justice."

Although Azim was overwhelmed with grief and loss, he felt as though he were in a trance, receiving strength from a higher power.

The next few days continued in this blur. Relatives arrived at Azim's house, and the homicide detectives continued gathering information. The phone rang endlessly while newspaper and television reporters tried to get statements from the family. Members of Azim's mosque flooded the house with food and prayers. Azim was grateful for all of the support, yet he felt emotionally paralyzed, as if he were in the middle of a terrible nightmare and couldn't wake up. Although his waking hours were torturous, he had trouble falling asleep to drift away from the pain of loss. His days became physically

Tariq and Azim Khamisa

and mentally exhausting as his thoughts constantly cycled through details of Tariq's death.

Four days after Tariq's death, there was a memorial in San Diego. Although the burial would be a few days later in Vancouver, this gathering of 250 people allowed those who had known Tariq in San Diego to remember him as the kindhearted person he was. All along, Azim tried to make sense of what seemed like a senseless act of violence. Just before the shooting, when Azim was in Mexico, Mirtila, his now ex-girlfriend, had given him a book. Although there was no way he could have predicted that it would soon apply to his life, the book was called *The Tibetan Book of Living and Dying*.

A chapter in the book discussed the Tibetan Buddhist concept of a *bardo*. This word was put together to signify a transitional state of life. "Bar" means "in between," and "do" means "suspended." Azim realized Tariq's soul was in a bardo. However, Azim's life was also in a bardo, and he wondered how this transitional state was going to play out for him and his family.

These were the thoughts running around in Azim's head when he entered the mosque in Vancouver for Tariq's funeral. Although he had never experienced such a depth of sadness, Azim felt oddly calm while listening to the chanting of the salawat during the Ismaili service. The purpose of the salawat was to help Tariq's soul pass into its next phase. Everyone in the prayer hall recites it in unison. The chanting, which lasted for 2½ hours, brought a sense of calm that he hadn't experienced in the five days since he had learned about Tariq's death. The chanting of 1,200 people was electrifying. The salawat gave Azim the strength to carry his son and bury him in his grave. His family surrounded him while carrying the litter, the flat piece of wood on which Tariq's body was laid. Azim took the two posts in the front, his brother supported the back, and his nephews were alongside so Tariq was not alone.

According to tradition, only the men went to the grave where Tariq was to be buried. When Azim and other family members arrived at the gravesite, they saw the empty earth where Tariq would be laid to rest. It was Azim's responsibility to enter the grave first and accept Tariq's body as it was lowered into the ground. As he received his son in the grave, Azim's resolve weakened and thoughts began to cycle in his mind. *I should be buried alongside my son. I will stay in this grave with Tariq.* Living in the world without his son felt too heavy to bear, and he didn't have the strength or desire to lift himself from the grave. Dan, Azim's close friend, could see what Azim was feeling and eventually pulled him out of the grave. Azim felt empty. He went through the motions alongside the other men to throw a spadeful of earth over Tariq's body, which was shrouded in a white unstitched cloth. Once Tariq was formally laid to rest in the ground, Azim returned to the prayer room where a traditional lunch was served. The room was filled with people, but Azim felt empty.

After the funeral, the reality sank back in, and Azim finally began to feel some anger. Before Tariq's murder, he was elated that Tariq and Tasreen were able to become United States citizens. After the murder, he started to question the society in which he had chosen to raise a family. Azim asked himself how a 14-year-old child could kill his son? For a brief moment, he contemplated moving away from the country he loved and called home. However, he quickly realized that running away wasn't the answer. Instead, he knew he would have to find a way to channel his anger. For three weeks after the murder, Azim kept the idea in the back of his mind: He needed to give meaning to Tariq's life, but he wasn't ready to act yet. At this point, with the murder so raw in his memory, even daily life was a struggle. Some days it took all of his energy to just get out of bed.

Before Tariq's death, Azim's work as an international banker took him around the world, and he dedicated all his energy to work, no matter how many hours were needed to close deals. After Tariq's death, he felt that his work had no purpose. He wondered if his life had a purpose. Before he felt ready to go back to work full time, Azim had to travel to Bulgaria to close a business deal he couldn't ignore. No one else at his firm was close enough to the deal, so in spite of his son's recent death, he had to travel. In those five days in another country, Azim hit his lowest point.

It was late winter in Bulgaria, windy and cold. Even though a doctor had prescribed sleeping pills, Azim wasn't sleeping. He passed the nights by walking for hours in no particular direction. When he couldn't walk anymore, he would take a taxi back to the hotel and repeat the pattern the next night. Thoughts of suicide crossed his mind because he couldn't imagine ever finding joy in his life again. Food didn't appeal to him, and at the end of the five days, Azim returned to the U.S. looking frail. He barely recognized himself in the mirror.

When he returned home, Azim got back on a plane to fly to Vancouver for the 40-day prayers that would take place in their mosque. According to Azim's Ismaili Muslim faith, prayers are recited at the funeral, on the 10th day after the death, and on the 30th day. However, the most significant prayers are recited on the 40th day. His faith held that the soul remained close to loved ones while they were grieving. After 40 days, a soul is believed to have moved to a new consciousness in preparation of its journey in the next world. Grieving past this time could hinder the soul's journey.

In late February, as they were nearing the 40-day mark, one of the leaders in the mosque came to Azim's mother's home and spoke directly to Azim. In the Ismaili faith, people serve in different types of leadership roles. Some become spiritual leaders or guides to support other members of the faith for however long they may need it. The spiritual leader that visited Azim's mother's home had been invited for dinner after the 40-day prayers. He introduced himself, and the two men learned that they shared the same name — Azim. The mosque leader opened the conversation with a statement to Tariq's father.

"The quality of the rest of your life depends on how you respond to this tragedy."

He paused to let that sink in before continuing. "It is human to grieve. But I recommend that you break the paralysis of grief and find a good deed to do in Tariq's name. Compassionate acts undertaken in the name of the departed are spiritual currency, which will transfer to Tariq's soul and provide high-octane fuel to help speed his journey."

Azim connected with the concept of "spiritual currency," and he knew that he would have to find a way to ensure that Tariq's journey could continue.

These words stayed with Azim even though he hadn't been ready to act on them in February. However, in April, after the 40 days, Azim knew it was time to do the inner work necessary to be able to do the outer work and undertake a good deed in Tariq's name. It started with a four-day trip to Mammoth Mountain, where his sole purpose was to calm his inner turmoil and start the work necessary to help Tariq move into the next life. A friend had lent Azim his condo for the short trip. He was completely isolated except for the servers at the restaurant, where he dined alone.

Azim thought about the last time he had seen Tariq. They met at their favorite breakfast restaurant, the Hob Nob Hill Restaurant, close to Tariq's apartment. They discussed a recent trip Azim had taken to India. Before he left for India, Tariq asked his dad to bring him back a rug. At breakfast, Azim gave Tariq the perfect green rug he had found for him in the city of Agra. They both ordered corned beef hash and eggs, and they talked about Tariq's relationship with Jennifer. The two college students were in love and had been thinking seriously about leaving San Diego to pursue Tariq's passion for photography outside of California — maybe in New York where Jennifer had a good friend. The last breakfast conversation was casual, and to Azim it seemed like lifetimes had passed since he shared that moment with his son.

As Azim reflected on this, he also felt regret. He asked himself, *Why didn't I make more time for Tariq? Why did I keep myself so busy with work?* This line of thought could take him to a dark place, and every time he started thinking this way, he tried to pull himself away from the path of regret to instead focus on the present.

At Mammoth, Azim saw his life heading down a different path than originally envisioned. He envisioned that instead of making Tony his enemy as the boy who had killed Tariq, Azim could take on the societal issue that had created Tony as his enemy. Azim could focus on fighting the peer pressure that forces many young men and women to choose gangs, crime, drugs, alcohol and weapons.

Azim felt his purpose shift from focusing on work to focusing on what happened the night of the shooting and figuring out how to grow from Tariq's murder. To do this, Azim needed more information about what happened that night. Once he started exploring this in more depth, he began to learn a great deal about Tony's background. He learned about where Tony grew up and the trauma he had experienced at a young age when his favorite cousin had been killed. Azim also learned about Ples, Tony's grandfather, who had been raising him. All of this information and more details about the night of the shooting surfaced from a filmmaker, Mike Reynolds. Reynolds was able to interview Tony 22 times between his arrest and the court hearing. The controversy over Tony and whether he should be tried as an adult delayed his hearing for almost 2½ years. In that time, the entire course of Azim's life had been changed.

It was common for Azim's mind to wander from thinking about Tariq to thinking about Tony, the 14-year-old who had killed him. As his thoughts drifted to Tony, they also drifted to Tony's grandfather, Ples. He wondered whether Ples felt the same sense of loss from losing Tony to the court system. Although Tony was still alive, his life was over as he knew it. Azim couldn't understand the senselessness of it all. How could they live in a nation where gun violence claimed the life of a young person every 90 minutes?

Ples Felix and Azim Khamisa during the early years of TKF

As Azim continued to do his inner work, he kept coming back to one question: *How am I going to get through the rest of my life?* He remembered what the leader in his mosque had said about undertaking compassionate acts in Tariq's name and turning this into spiritual currency. He knew he had to find a way to give meaning to Tariq's death. The solitude in Mammoth allowed Azim to clear his thoughts enough to get the seed of an idea. After four days of introspection, Azim left Mammoth with a little bit of hope and the spark of an idea for a foundation to help young people like Tony. He would call it the Tariq Khamisa Foundation.

If he created a foundation that performed compassionate deeds in Tariq's name, it could build up spiritual currency so Tariq could complete his journey in the next world in a rocket. Creating this nonprofit organization could also give Azim strength and a renewed purpose in life. The vision for TKF would be a win for Tariq, a win for Azim, and a win for society. When Azim returned from Mammoth Mountain, he jumped into action to start building TKF with his friend Dan and many other well-wishers.

The first step for Azim was to share his idea to start a foundation in Tariq's name with as many people as possible who might support him. As he met with people, he explained that the foundation could prevent other parents from having to know the pain of losing a child to violence. The more people he talked to, the more people wanted to get involved. Azim finally had clarity, and it felt as if the confusion he was living in was finally lifted. Within a couple of months, friends and acquaintances had all gotten behind Azim's idea to create the Tariq Khamisa Foundation. And he was certain that naming the foundation for his son could provide the spiritual currency to help Tariq on the next part of his journey.

In October, eight months after Tariq's death, TKF had its first meeting. Since the foundation did not have a building yet, the first meeting took place in Azim's townhouse. Fifty people crammed into the small space to commit themselves to the mission of TKF. The prosecutor assigned to Tony's case, Peter Deddeh, gave the opening speech and then introduced Azim. He said he had never seen anything like this after a violent crime had been committed. The community organized around a desire to prevent a senseless crime like this from happening again. Some people wept listening to Azim's story and other stories connected to Tariq's death. By the end of the night, the Tariq Khamisa Foundation was officially born. To do this work well and completely, though, one piece was still missing for Azim. After everyone left his house that evening, Azim asked the prosecuting attorney if he could arrange for Azim to meet Tony's grandfather, Ples Felix.

Peter Deddeh had prosecuted many cases in his career. He knew Azim was choosing an unusual way to handle his son's death. He agreed to call Tony's attorney. Deddeh and public defender Henry Corker agreed that they and Azim would meet at Corker's office to discuss whether it was appropriate to set up a meeting with Ples and Azim.

When Azim arrived at the office, he was surprised to find Ples sitting at Henry Corker's desk. In addition to the attorneys, Mike Reynolds, the filmmaker who had spent so much time with Tony after the arrest, had escorted Azim into the room. Although they were never able to find the funds to produce the documentary, the relationship that Mike developed with Tony gave him another person in his corner. Azim entered the room and immediately made eye contact with Ples. Everything else in the room stood still. Azim walked over to Ples and extended his hand. Ples shook his hand, and the two men sat down next to each other. Azim felt a connection with Ples at a soulular level, as they were both deeply spiritual men. Ples later said he felt the same connection.

Azim began the conversation. "I am not here in the spirit of retribution. I feel that we both lost a son, and there are victims at both ends of the gun. I have started a foundation because I can't bring my son back, but my hope is that we can stop kids from killing other kids. I don't want other parents to go through what we have gone through."

With pure sincerity in his voice, Ples offered his deepest condolences to the Khamisa family and said the family was in his prayers and meditations every day. Azim acknowledged the loss Tony's family had faced.

Maybe it was the bond of being the male family members who were most deeply connected to the shooting. Or maybe it was the bond of sharing a deep spirituality in prayer and meditation, but it was obvious to everyone in the room that Azim and Ples did indeed seem bonded. Ples listened to Azim's vision of the foundation in Tariq's name, and Ples said he would help in any way he could. As the two men continued their conversation about the foundation, Azim decided it was time to ask Ples for something he knew would take a lot of bravery. The second meeting of TKF was to take place the following week. Tariq's mother, sister, grandparents, aunts and cousins would be there. Azim asked Ples if he would come and speak at the meeting. To Azim's surprise, Ples agreed.

When the day came, Ples walked bravely into the room. They both talked about the tragedy that had happened, and Ples made a public commitment to the Tariq Khamisa Foundation. He ended his remarks with a question for the audience: "I will commit to this effort. Will you?" Azim knew from the group's response that he and Ples would make this journey together through their new organization.

The next few months involved fundraising and connecting with people willing to help with all of the business and financial details of starting a foundation. Even though TKF was a nonprofit, starting it came with many costs. Once they had raised a little money, the foundation was able to start building programs for kids. Six months after the first meeting, TKF hired its first full-time employee. A local law firm donated office space. News coverage generated community support. People who had followed the story of the youngest person to be tried as an adult in California were moved by the response of the Khamisa family as well as Ples.

Members of the foundation knew the audience for this work was schoolchildren, and they wanted to spread a message of nonviolence. However, it wasn't until they had booked their first program at Birney Elementary School that they had to decide *how* they were

The day Azim Khamisa met Tony Hicks for the first time, accompanied by Ples Felix

going to spread this message. A counselor from school reached out to TKF because Tony had been a student there. Students didn't know what to think about Tony, and this led TKF to come up with the concept for their first program. Although the members of the foundation had many discussions about how they could craft their message to the students, they decided on an interactive assembly. The most powerful part of the program took place after Tariq and Tony's story was told, and then Ples and Azim walked out together and sat side by side in front of the students. The main message of the program was that violence caused traumatic damage that could never be undone. However, they also stressed that violence was a chosen behavior. Everyone in the audience had it in their control to choose to be nonviolent.

Azim drove this point home to the students with powerful words in his speech at Birney Elementary:

66

"There's nothing more powerful in this world than a child's life. To me, a child's life is more precious than even my own. You see, I know this from personal experience. Seventeen months ago my only son, Tariq, was shot and killed. He was delivering a pizza. I'll never forget hearing that on the phone. At first I could not believe it was true. But after I talked to his girlfriend, Jennifer, the truth began to sink in. He was gone — gone forever. I would never see him or touch him or hear him laugh again.

I didn't know how I would be strong enough to call my daughter and tell her that her brother was dead. ... It seemed impossible to me that four teenagers would surround my son to try to rob him of a pizza, and that one of them would shoot him dead for a pizza. I felt numb for weeks. The pain was too great.

When my feelings slowly started to come back, one of the first things I felt was anger. ... With the death of my son, I felt my life had lost all its purpose. I was angry at America. I thought about running away to another part of the world. But I realized I loved my adopted country, and I had to stay and fight. I had to face reality. But how?

This is where you children come in. Sometimes we all get caught in situations where others do things we can't control. That's how it was with Tariq's murder. But if you think about it, we do have control over how we respond. We always have a choice. You see, I chose to turn my grief into positive action.

In our country, we lose 13 kids a day to a gun. And on both ends of the gun there is a tragedy. That's why I decided to reach out to the family of Tony Hicks, who pulled the trigger on Tariq, and Tony's grandfather, Ples Felix.

... Reaching out to Ples was not an easy thing for me to do. Many people thought I should seek revenge, get an eye for an eye. But what would that accomplish? Would it bring Tariq back? It would only continue the violence that took Tariq's life. Answering violence with violence won't change anything.

All you boys and girls here, you all deserve to be able to walk without fear. You deserve to have your dreams come true. To raise families of your own. You deserve ... a future. We adults of this world have done a pretty lousy job of making this happen so far. We need you to help us. Will you do your best to help stop violence?"

As Azim finished speaking, he looked at all the eyes intently staring at him from the audience. The students all paused at first as his question hung in the air. Azim spoke again, "Do you all promise to try?"

This time the students' voices came together for an overpowering response, "Yes!"

Azim's forgiveness journey started the night Tariq was killed. He had gone from living an exciting, full life to what felt like no life at all. He knew he couldn't dwell in that heavy feeling. Once his spiritual mentor said the rest of Azim's life depended on how he chose to respond to the tragedy, Azim found purpose again. He began to dig himself slowly out of the pit he was in. In his heart he knew that grieving would impede Tariq's spiritual journey, but it took him some time to begin to bounce back in his heart. An idea had popped into his mind: What if Tony wasn't Azim's enemy? What if Azim made his enemy the drugs, alcohol and gangs that led kids to fall through the cracks?

Through the Tariq Khamisa Foundation, Azim has not only personally healed, but the organization has been able to reach more than 600,000 kids and many million other youth and adults through media and Azim's extensive international speaking and writing of five books — to teach the power of choosing forgiveness over revenge. Tariq continued on his own journey, but he left his name and spirit as a gift for his family and society. The Tariq Khamisa Foundation has been given a mandate to perform compassionate deeds rooted in love, not revenge.

Addendum: Jennifer

After Tariq's death, Jennifer had to clean out the apartment they had shared together. Azim told her to please keep anything she wanted. She kept some of Tariq's journals and photographs he had taken. She also kept the green rug that Tariq had asked his father to bring him from India. She felt connected to Tariq on that rug because he had loved it so much.

Azim came to know Jennifer well the last couple of years of Tariq's life. Tariq and Jennifer shared an apartment, but they also had a key to Azim's townhome. Sometimes they would spend the whole weekend at Azim's home, and whenever Tariq and Jennifer were together, they were very affectionate with each other. When Azim and Tariq met for meals, Jennifer always came up as a topic of conversation. It was evident through what Tariq said, but also *how* he talked about her, that he loved Jennifer very much. He told his father they were planning to get married once they moved away from San Diego and were settled.

Tariq Khamisa and his fiancé, Jennifer

Forgiveness was not Jennifer's path. In the early years, when Azim asked her if she would like to be involved with the foundation, she responded angrily.

"How can you forgive someone who killed Tariq?" she asked.

When Azim said he was going to leave Tony to a higher power, she made it clear that she couldn't move on in the same way. She coped with the grief by turning to drugs.

Azim reflected on the last time he had seen Jennifer — three years after Tariq's death. They kept in touch through letters before they saw each other in person the final time. Usually they wrote a letter around Christmas. However, it had been a long time since they had seen each other, and Azim wanted to meet up with her in person. Since she had moved to Northern California, Azim decided to visit her in San Francisco. They agreed to meet in town, but Jennifer was 2½ hours late to their arranged meeting time. As soon as he saw her, he could tell she was high on something. Although she was there across from him, it was if she weren't really present.

At one point in the conversation, Azim was straightforward. "You have to get some help for this."

"I know I do, Azim," Jennifer responded. "I'm going to move back in with my parents so I can."

True to her word, Jennifer began living with her parents. With their support she was able to kick her drug habit. One of the most powerful letters Azim received from her came soon after their face-to-face meeting.

Dear Azim,

I hope it hasn't been too long, but I've finally gotten to a place in my life where I'm able to actually sit down and let you know that I'm thinking of you. It's been, what, three and a half years now, and you'd think it would be over by now, but it's not. At least for me it isn't. I hope you have been well and have moved on from this experience as I have tried to. Although I haven't kept up to date with the foundation or your work, I hope it's doing as well as it was the last time I spoke with you. And better, I hope it's helping you to heal as time passes on.

I'm not sure if you knew, but I've been dwelling in my pain since I left San Diego and have not found it within myself to return until fairly recently. I found a way to escape from all that had happened through an addiction to heroin and about a year and a half ago went to rehab to try and recover. Unfortunately my addiction was not all that I had to recover from and the rest was too hard for me to let go of at that time.

I left rehab after about five months and have returned home a couple of times since then. I'm now living at home with my parents, in therapy and starting to come to terms with my loss.

I have not been in contact for reasons I cannot explain. I have felt that my healing process was one that had to be done separately to experience the full magnitude of my loss. I am writing this in hopes that I may in the future begin to reestablish some correspondence as I think of you and your family often and wish to send you all my love.

Sincerely,

Jennifer

Azim realized after talking to Jennifer's father much later, that her sobriety was short-lived.

Ten years after Tariq's death, Jennifer's father, Bruce, called Azim. He wanted to know where Tariq was buried. To Azim, it seemed like an odd question. Azim explained that it would be hard to find his grave since Tariq had been buried in Vancouver.

"Bruce, Tariq died 10 years ago. Why do you want to know where he is buried?" At this point, Azim hadn't heard from Jennifer in a few years, and the last time they had seen each other was the weekend Azim flew her to San Diego.

"How is Jennifer doing?" Azim asked.

Bruce paused before answering. "Jennifer commited suicide three years ago. She died from a heroin overdose. It would have been her 30th birthday this year. She was her happiest when she was with Tariq. We would like to sprinkle her ashes on Tariq's grave."

And so, on Jennifer's 30th birthday, she was laid to rest with Tariq in Vancouver. She never reached a level of forgiveness that could move her past her grief.

Ples Felix

"Forgiveness is a joyful exercise you do for yourself to build a better person. When you forgive, you make more room for love and compassion."
— *Ples Felix*

Ples learned very early in life that the world was filled with conflict. When he was growing up, Ples knew that trying to go unnoticed was a sure way to become a target. Ples was labeled "the yellow boy" in his neighborhood because he had light skin. He felt highlighted in a background of blackness. He was especially a target of the older kids in the neighborhood who sometimes tried to push him into fights with other boys. When he was playing in the neighborhood, he was always on alert for a potential conflict.

Even though Ples didn't want to fight with others, his father had a different view of conflict. His dad insisted that Ples learn how to defend himself so he could resolve conflicts this way if he had to. Ples had

Ples Felix and Tony Hicks

many fights until he learned there were other ways to solve problems. He learned that the best way to stay away from fights was to find and show empathy for the instigator. If he had an understanding of the conflict, and let the other person know he understood, this could keep both people out of a fight. Ples practiced and strengthened his empathy muscle so that by the time he was a teenager, he was finding ways to avoid fights in his conflict-filled world.

Even as an adult, Ples found it was important to keep his empathy muscle strong. This empathy kicked in as soon as Tony was arrested after the murder. Ples knew he would need to support both Tony and his daughter (Tony's mother). He would have to find a way to acknowledge and clarify his own emotions so he could think about next steps for Tony. Based on his background in the Army, Ples knew that if he could remain emotionally balanced, he would be able to make clear decisions. This clarity was necessary to be able to support Tony, who was now in the crosshairs of the criminal justice system. Ples used both meditation and yoga to stay balanced in this incredibly stressful time. Some days, Ples did two or even three full sessions of yoga to remain clear, mentally and emotionally.

While details surrounding the murder continued to unfold, Ples balanced his internal positive energy with support for his family. He advocated for Tony and helped him as he navigated the legal system. He supported his daughter and made sure she received daily updates on her son and the case. He also maintained compassion for the Khamisa family, who had experienced an immense loss. Navigating the legal system with Tony was new for Ples, and this took a different type of energy.

Ples knew he needed to find a defense attorney for Tony. Because he could not afford to hire an expensive defense attorney for a kid accused of murder, he went directly to the Public Defender's Office. The first person he met there was Jeff Riley, a well-known public defender. Riley had read about the case in the papers by the time Ples came in to see him. They discussed the implications of this case as Tony might become the first juvenile tried as an adult in California since the new law had taken effect in January.

Riley looked at Ples directly when he said, "Mr. Felix, I'd love to be able to take this case on, but I am so overburdened right now. There is no way I could be of service to your grandson." Before Ples could interject, he said, "But I've got a great partner here, and his name is Henry Corker."

Riley's face lit up when he mentioned Henry Corker's name, and Ples could see how sincere he was in his praise of his colleague. The tone of his voice and his sincere expression gave Ples a great sense of confidence. From their brief interaction, Ples could tell that the Public Defender's Office was deeply invested in supporting Tony. Soon after this initial meeting, Henry Corker and Ples met for the first time.

Henry explained the urgency of the situation. "We understand from Juvenile Hall that Tony is in bravado mode, and we need to cure that before he steps into the court. He can't go in front of *this* judge with that kind of attitude. Can you talk to Tony about this?"

Ples understood the false bravado of his grandson. It looked like a little kid trying to be a big kid in Juvenile Hall. It sounded like Tony defensively blaming the murder on the stupidity of the pizza man for not giving up his pizza. Tony had adopted the lifestyle of a gangster, but that's not who he was. Ples knew Tony would be tried as an adult, and Henry explained the seriousness of the situation.

"Hey, look," Henry said softly. "There are two ways this can go here. Tony can continue down this bravado course. If he wants to go into Judge Weber's court with this, she will throw him in prison for the rest of his natural life." Henry paused to make sure option one was clear.

"Or he can go in and be the person that shows contrition and takes responsibility and seeks the forgiveness of the people that he harmed and hurt. He can address the court with a commitment of not being that person that killed Tariq Khamisa ever again."

Ples understood the weight of the options Henry laid in front of him. As the public defender, Henry was able to arrange for Ples and Tony to meet at Juvenile Hall the next evening to talk through the options. Ples asked Henry if he could bring two pieces of fruit into the meeting room, his tradition when talking with his grandson. Henry agreed, and they decided that after Henry greeted Tony, he would leave the grandfather and grandson to talk in privacy.

Ples and Tony met in a large concrete holding room at Juvenile Hall. Concrete benches lined the wall, and bright lights illuminated the room. This was different from the open space where Ples would normally meet Tony.

After Tony greeted the lawyer, he sat next to his grandfather on a concrete bench. As soon as Henry left the room, Tony withered. He jumped into Ples' lap and started crying. "Daddy, Daddy. I'm so sorry. I didn't mean to hurt anybody. I didn't mean to shoot anybody. I'm so sorry."

Ples consoled him while he responded in a warm tone. "I understand, son. I know you didn't want to hurt anybody. I know you were angry. I know you were upset," he said. Tony continued to cry and Ples let the words sink in.

"Now you have to take responsibility for what you did." This sent Tony into deeper sobbing. Eventually Ples continued. "Know that I love you and your mom loves you, but you have to do the right thing here. This is something you have to do. I can't tell you how to do it. I can't tell you what to do, but I know you know what to do, to do the right thing."

Ples handed Tony a handkerchief, and it seemed to make him feel a little better. Tony slowly stood and moved over to sit next to his grandfather. Ples held out the two pieces of fruit.

"Let me have the orange."

Ples handed his grandson the orange and kept the apple. Tony peeled the orange in silence and started to eat. Ples could feel Tony firming up next to him, and Tony looked very different from the withered body he was a few moments ago. Ples listened as Tony spoke. "Daddy, I know what to do. I'll do the right thing. I know what I need to do."

Henry was invited back into the room with papers for Tony to sign acknowledging that he would be tried as an adult and that he

Ples Felix visiting adult Tony Hicks in prison

had to make a plea in court the next day. Tony and Ples read the document together, and Ples asked him, "Do you understand what this is all about?"

Tony responded, "Yeah. I'm actually signing to go into court tomorrow and be tried as an adult." His voice was quiet but resolved.

Henry reassured them that he would be with them in court every step of the way. "I'll look forward to being there early tomorrow morning. I'll be right there with you."

Henry felt relieved that Ples was able to break down Tony's defensiveness to ready himself for court. Ples felt relieved, as well. Tony had not only dropped his false bravado, but he was able to unburden himself with the truth. This allowed him to prepare for court being true to himself as Tony Hicks, not the person who carelessly shot a pizza man.

By the time Tony entered the court hearing the next day, Ples was sitting in the first row, in the chair closest to the entry gate. He wanted to make sure Tony saw him sitting right there and knew he was supporting him. Tony's mother sat behind him with two of her girlfriends. Ples knew that decisions made that day would change their lives, and he knew Tony was very likely going to prison.

The hearing started, and Ples could only watch it unfold from his seat. When Tony was asked directly how he was pleading, he read a response. Tony, in a blue prison jumpsuit, sat to Henry Corker's right, and he looked out of place — a child in an adult's world. As he began speaking, the sincere emotion in his voice came through clearly. Tony had written his speech on a yellow legal pad. As Ples listened, he realized that Tony's words reflected much of what he had learned from living with Ples and watching him work. Ples often had to practice speeches to give to City Council, and he would practice at home. Tony had his paper in front of him as a reference, but he spent most of his speech with his head up, looking Judge Weber in the eye. To be able to read parts from the paper but then articulate the rest with his head raised further confirmed Tony's sincerity. At the end of his speech, Tony said, through his tears, *"My grandfather promised me that he will be Mr. Khamisa's friend and help him in any way he can for the rest of his life. I am very sorry for what I have done. Thank you for giving me the chance to speak."*

After the statement, the judge announced Tony's sentence: 25 years to life in prison. Tony hugged his mother goodbye before an officer led him away. The sentencing was over. Ples felt conflicting emotions. He was proud that Tony had demonstrated his true character with honesty and remorse in the court at such a young age. At the same time, he naturally felt low watching his daughter as she witnessed her baby sentenced to prison.

Although the sentencing seemed in many ways to be the expected outcome, the impact was still settling on Ples and the rest of Tony's circle of support. Ples had not only been thinking about Tony in this process, but he had been thinking constantly about the Khamisa family. Ples had already mentioned to Henry Corker that he would like to meet with Mr. Khamisa. There was no expectation that Ples would be able to communicate directly with the Khamisa family. However, he was hopeful that if Henry Corker could communicate his intent with the Khamisas' attorney, perhaps a meeting could be arranged with Azim, Tariq's father. To Ples, this felt very pressing.

A few months after the hearing, Ples received the call he was hoping for. Henry said, "Look, there may be an opportunity here to meet Mr. Khamisa. But he won't be alone. He will more than likely be with other people. Is that OK with you?"

Ples said it didn't matter who was with Mr. Khamisa because he just wanted to express his heartfelt condolences and offer the family support in whatever way he could.

Soon, Henry called again. He didn't give Ples many details, and Ples didn't press the issue.

"There is going to be a meeting in my office. You should try to make it a point to be present," Henry said, without providing any more information.

Ples said he would be there, and he believed this might be his chance to speak to the Khamisas' attorney to request a meeting with Mr. Khamisa.

During his adult life, Ples always made it a point to be early to meetings. He liked to show up at least five minutes early, but sometimes more, so that he could settle into the space and make sure he was prepared for the meeting. On this day, Ples was early and sitting at Henry's desk when Azim stepped through the door, accompanied by two burly men. Neither Azim nor Ples knew the other would be there. Both men wore a slightly bemused look.

Ples couldn't help but smile as he walked toward Azim. He knew that the moment was serious, yet he felt an immediate warmth from Azim.

As Ples reached Azim, he held out his hand and said, "I'm pleased to meet you. I want to express my sympathies and condolences on the loss of your son at the hands of my grandson, and I want to support you and your family." The largest man accompanying Azim seemed to relax his body a little as he stood behind them. The tension left the room.

Azim responded, "I don't hold any animosity. Our kids are out here killing kids, and something has to be done about that." He continued, "I formed a foundation in the name of my son, and we are having our second meeting soon. I'd like to invite you to it. Will you come?"

Ples didn't have to think about the proposition before he responded gratefully, "That's an answer to my prayer. I will be there."

Azim held Ples' gaze and said, "My mom will be there. My dad will be there. My brother and sister will be there also."

Ples nodded and reaffirmed his response. "I look forward to being there."

The two fathers discussed some of the details before saying goodbye.

Although Ples had not entered the meeting feeling overly burdened, he left the meeting feeling inspired and lighter. In addition to the gratitude he felt for Azim, he felt the sincerity in being welcomed into the house, which might normally be considered enemy territory. They hadn't talked about forgiving each other or Tony; yet Ples felt a great sense of support for Tony from an unexpected place — Tariq's family.

Azim Khamisa and Ples Felix, 25 years of promoting forgiveness, peace and hope

The court had already decided Tony's future; he was going to prison for a very long time. However, now something good might come out of this tragedy for the Khamisa family. Ples felt honored and inspired to be welcomed into a family setting and to be a part of this.

Ples carried this feeling of hope and optimism into the meeting, which took place at Azim's house. When he entered the space for the first time, he wanted to make sure that the way he carried himself showed that he was open and supportive of the Khamisa family. The living room had been set up to maximize space for all the people standing and sitting in every available area. Furniture had been removed or pushed all the way to the edges of the space. Azim had placed a lectern in the foyer of the living room. There was a small step down into the living room, and the lectern was elevated on this step to give the impression of a stage.

To prepare, Ples made notes about what he hoped to share with the Khamisas about tragedy and how it affects everyone. When given the chance to speak, Ples started in his calming voice, "I am really honored and thankful to be invited here into Azim Khamisa's house. I am hopeful that the work we do in this newly formed foundation will prevent kids from harming other kids like my grandson harmed Tariq. I'm very committed to do all I can to be of support to the family and to our kids."

As he looked out into the faces of people in the room, he saw no hostility, only loss. He could feel sorrow in the room, but he felt no anger. This was the first time Ples fully understood how Azim's forgiveness was real. Ples felt it in the room, and he saw it reflected in the faces of Tariq's relatives. The way they were dealing with trauma and loss was an inspiration. Although Ples had forgiven Tony quickly, the forgiveness in the room showed Ples what to do with that forgiveness for a greater impact.

When Ples looked back at all of the trauma that Tony experienced in his childhood, he saw how Tony's decision to shoot Tariq and this trauma were interlaced. He knew that childhood trauma, if left unresolved, could become a bomb waiting to explode. The fuses might be very long, but they continue to burn down. Even though Ples enrolled Tony in therapy, the fuse continued to burn, and it exploded the day Tony decided to run away from home. The fuse had been burning for years, though — ever since he was a little kid. It was impossible to separate the nature of Tony's childhood and the nature of his actions. Ples had to forgive Tony in the context of understanding his journey.

For Ples, forgiving himself was and is a longer process. He felt the weight of what Tony had done on a personal level, and he felt that in many respects he had failed Tony. When Tony came to live with him, Ples parented in a way that made sense to him. With his military background, he wanted to provide Tony with discipline, but he realized that this was trying to fit Tony into a lifestyle that didn't fit for him. That ended up backfiring for Tony, who needed more compassion and more opportunities to express himself. The reality was that Tony wanted to live with his mom. That wasn't an option. Instead, he got the strict household of his grandfather.

Ples had already been practicing forgiving himself for 25 years before Tony shot Tariq. When he was discharged from the Army in 1970, he carried the destructive memories of combat with him. These memories became a burden he couldn't shake. He knew joining the Army had been honorable. He knew he fought to serve his country. He was honorably discharged. Yet this understanding of honor was in conflict with his memories of what actually happens when fighting a war. After leaving the Army, Ples couldn't ignore the weight of these burdens he shouldered from years of war. He had to look deep inside and confront them. But most important, he had to commit to never repeat them again. Only then was he able to unburden himself.

After the Army, a lot of this self-reflection and eventual forgiveness came through meditation, which became a lifestyle for Ples. Through this, he felt his burdens diminish since the night Tony took Tariq's life. Although the burdens haven't completely left, they have shrunk to the size of a pea. When he meditates, positive and negative feelings show up as colors. He sees negativity in a deep red and positive in a light blue. By visualizing negative feelings, it's easier for him to notice them getting smaller.

As he diminished the deep red over the years through meditation, Ples made more room for love and compassion. Making room for love has helped him be stronger in difficult times. This path to forgiveness has helped Ples build himself as a better person, and although the path continues, it has allowed him to give and welcome joy into his heart.

From the moment he met Azim, Ples made it known that he would be available to support him and the work of the Tariq Khamisa Foundation. They join each other on stage across the world when schools invite them to speak. When Ples is introduced, he is identified as the man whose grandson killed the other man's son. And then they share a stage to tell their story with nothing but compassion and support for each other. For Ples, this journey toward forgiveness has put him in front of thousands of people at Azim's side to show that young people can choose peace and nonviolence. Their journeys of forgiveness that brought them together have transformed thousands of lives, and the lives of Ples' and Azim's families.

Ples Felix and Azim Khamisa celebrating Tariq Khamisa Day on March 6, 2019

87

Almas Khamisa

"Everyone around us, no matter their age, has all kinds of difficulties and conflicts in their lives. And we are not supposed to bury our heads in the sand because of this. We are supposed to face these conflicts in whatever positive way you can: through dialogue, through interactions, through learning about stories and what the outcomes could be from these tragic stories you see around the world. You can live by example."
— Almas Khamisa

Tariq's mother, Almas, was in Vancouver the night her son was killed, but she didn't hear about it until the next morning. She had driven with Tasreen to spend some time in Vancouver while Azim's father had open-heart surgery. The families had remained close even after Almas and Azim's divorce. Originally, the families lived in the

Almas Khamisa with her children Tasreen and Tariq Khamisa

same small town in Kenya, and that's where they met. And although they didn't plan it, both families ended up in Vancouver when they left Kenya to seek political asylum. Tasreen was with Azim's family and Almas was with her parents and brother when she got the call from Azim the morning after the shooting.

Azim's voice came across directly. "Tariq has been shot. He is dead."

Almas began screaming, and her brother and mother came running to her. She sank to her knees. The phone fell from her hand.

"Almas, what is it? What's going on? Is it your father-in-law?" her brother asked.

90

She continued screaming and responded, "No. Tariq. Tariq. Tariq ..."
Her brother asked again, "What happened?"
Eventually she was able to get out the words. "Tariq got killed."
Her brother took the phone from the floor and heard the limited
information Azim knew at this point. After sharing what he knew
with the people in the house, including Tasreen, Almas' brother began
calling relatives. Tasreen came over immediately and Almas sat down,
shocked, as people started to arrive. According to their religion, as soon
as someone dies, the spiritual journey of the soul has begun. Although
the grief and shock is there, everyone's main concern is the passage of
the soul. People were there to comfort Almas and Tasreen, but they
also reminded them that the focus was to rise above his death and
focus on his life and the journey he had embarked on after his death.

Even though she was in shock, Almas was engulfed with feelings
of love and support from everyone who had shown up, as if they were
holding her when it was hard to stand. Their faith taught them that
everyone is a spiritual being in a physical form for a short amount of
time. The physical being has a short life compared to the eternal life of
the soul. With everyone around, Almas slowly came to that realization.

Almas and Azim were asked to identify the body, and for Almas
it was important to see Tariq even though she knew it was going to
be incredibly hard. Her brother booked airline tickets for Almas
and Tasreen and brought them to the airport as soon as they were
able to get a flight to San Diego. In the airport, Tasreen had to hold
Almas at the ticket counter to keep her from crumbling to the floor.

In San Diego, the family went back to Azim's apartment where
Almas, still distraught, began piecing together bits of information
about Tariq's death. She knew Tariq had been shot, but the family
also learned that four people were involved in the shooting. She also
learned that they had shot Tariq over a pizza, and that the boys had

Almas and Tariq Khamisa at Tariq's high school graduation

all been arrested and connected to a gang. Within three days they found out that the boy who pulled the trigger was 14 years old.

Almas and Azim were finally allowed to see the body. Almas' grief was now joined by anger. She was angry that she had lost her son, that he was actually gone. Now and then she thought, *What did I do wrong?* She got stuck thinking about Tariq's decisions that night, and wondering why he wouldn't give up the pizza. Almas knew that Tariq was fearless. He had been fearless his whole life. She still had a vivid memory of Tariq saying, "Mom, watch me fly," and he would jump off a table or other furniture in the house. Almas thought Tariq had seen the boys as kids, not as real threats. If she was right, he wouldn't have given up a pizza to kids who had sent him to a fake address and then refused to pay. The senselessness of this made her anger well up.

She was angry at Tariq for refusing to give up the pizza. And she was angry at society. At the time, the United States was one of the most violent countries in the world. Almas asked herself, *How could we be so powerful and so violent at the same time?* However, her anger was never directed at Tony. Once she learned about Tony's childhood, there was no internal battle over forgiving him. These angry emotions never came up. Instead, the feelings were directed at a society in which a 14-year-old killed her son over a $10 pizza.

Between 1990 and 1995, violent crimes and murder spiked in San Diego. The most violent year for San Diego was 1993, when about 10 people in 1,000 were victims of violent crime. Although the murder rate in Los Angeles was three times higher than in San Diego, cities all over the country were reaching their peaks in the early 1990s. Part of the reason was drugs, specifically the growing availability of crack cocaine. This increase in drug use led to an increase in gang activity in San Diego, and new gangs were forming, like the one that Tony ran with.

Until now, Almas never thought about the growing violence in the U.S. Although she listened to the news, she heard about violence and paused to think how sad it was, but that was all. Before the shooting, they lived their relatively comfortable lives unaware of the growing gang activity across the country.

After the shooting, the whole family began to examine this larger problem in society. Quickly, Azim and Ples formed the foundation to address this problem. Eventually, Tasreen also had the courage to join the foundation to work on the problem of youth violence. However, Almas was unable to channel her grief in the same way. She was angry and grieving, and she mostly felt shut down. After the memorial services, Almas looked forward to going back to work. The only thing that brought her any comfort was being in a classroom with the young kids at the Montessori school where she worked. She was most comfortable with students younger than fourth grade. After Tariq's

93

Almas Khamisa
during her time as a teacher

death, Almas learned that students began joining gangs in fourth and fifth grade. One of the reasons she stayed at the Montessori school was that their focus was on educating the whole child. When students had conflicts in class, they went to a peace table in the room where they could resolve their conflicts.

When Almas returned to work, she learned that the entire staff had gone through grief counseling so they could support her. The staff became her family, and teaching made her stronger. On her first day back, she asked her students to sit in a circle so she could tell them what had happened to her son. Some of the students got up and hugged her. One said she shouldn't worry because her son was in heaven, and in heaven, Tariq was delivering a pizza. The earnest innocence of her students allowed her to move forward with her life.

Almas stayed in Seattle for five years after Tariq's death, in the same house where Tariq and Tasreen grew up. Tasreen moved in briefly after the shooting, but she eventually returned to San Diego. For the first few months, Almas couldn't even open the door to

Tariq's bedroom. She kept it shut until one day she was able to go inside, but still she was unable to remove anything. An unopened can of Pepsi remained next to Tariq's bed. Sometimes friends would come to the house and ask if they could help with Tariq's room. Almas said no. One friend asked if she could help put away Tariq's clothes. Almas said no. His bedroom stayed exactly as it was for five years. Sometime in the first year after the shooting, Almas' anger faded, but her grief and sadness remained. Everything in the house reminded her of Tariq. Finally, with a push from her daughter, Almas decided it was time to move away.

Tasreen encouraged her mom to either move to San Diego or back to Vancouver so she would have family nearby. The decision was easy. Almas told everyone that both of her kids were in San Diego, and she had decided to move there. Once she made this decision, she felt like she could finally breathe for the first time in five years. In the house and in the city, she had been so sad. Her future was in San Diego, and when she decided to move, she also started smiling again. Her work friends saw her transform. She described the feeling as heading out of a dark tunnel into the light for the first time since Tariq's death.

In San Diego, Almas went to where she found peace — elementary schools. She quickly had three job offers and chose a small nonprofit Catholic school. Although she wasn't Catholic, she felt like she needed some spirituality in her life, wherever that came from. She worked with 6- to 8-year-old students, the same age as her students in Seattle. The students were required to go to Mass twice a week, and the teachers went with them. Almas loved going to Mass. During the Christmas and Easter holidays, she attended Mass with the children as well. Her family in San Diego would ask her jokingly if she had given up on her Muslim faith. She responded with a laugh that this faith was what she needed at the moment. It was part of her day-

Photo of Almas Khamisa taken by Tariq Khamisa

to-day life, and she rose to new heights by singing in the choir with her students.

Once she had emerged from the dark tunnel into the light of San Diego, Almas felt a tremendous shift take place in her healing. Sometimes, the Tariq Khamisa Foundation invited her to speak at school assemblies. Even though it was painful, these assemblies were also healing. She told students how she reacted to her son's death. When they asked the middle school students to raise their hands if they had lost someone in their lives to violence, the rooms would fill with raised hands. Afterward, students came up to hug her. They said, "I promise you that I will never carry a gun." They seemed so innocent and even followed up sometimes with letters promising that they would choose a life of nonviolence. For Almas, seeing what the foundation was doing made her feel good, even though she couldn't commit to the same level as Azim, Tasreen or Ples.

Over the years, Azim and Tasreen had both met Tony at a time that felt right for them. Almas kept more of a distance, but she followed Tony's growth and progress. Tony wrote blogs and letters to students from prison, and Almas followed his writing. She watched him grow into a positive young man as he evolved in his search for his own forgiveness. After Tony's sentencing hearing, Almas watched the courtroom video. Tony sobbed as he read his statement. Almas knew she would never forget that video of Tony at the age of 16 in his sentencing hearing saying, "Please, I hope the Khamisa family will forgive me." From that day and after hearing about his childhood, she never had any bad feelings toward him. Almas has told Tasreen often that she plans to write to Tony and that, after 24 years, she looks forward to meeting him one day soon.

Almas is no longer angry at Tariq for refusing to give up the pizzas. Instead, she realized that Tariq was into something bigger than what happened that night. Through her faith, Almas recognized that life on Earth is short. She learned not to fall apart and instead grow from the pain. Tariq's journey was wrapped up in Tony's journey, and to Almas, Tony was just as important as Tariq in this lesson. She had to literally change her thinking from what she thought at first — that Tariq was just in the wrong place at the wrong time. Now she believes that Tariq was in the right place at the right time. Almas believes that at some point in another lifetime or spiritual plane, Tony and Tariq must have made a pact. This has led people who love both Tony and Tariq to do good work in Tariq's name.

Tasreen

"Forgiveness takes time. It's not overnight. It's a process. It's a journey. There is no right or wrong way in getting through it. It was the best gift I could give myself. It opened up a whole other world for me when I was able to do that."
— *Tasreen Khamisa*

Tasreen was at her grandmother's house in Vancouver when she got the news that her brother had been killed. Her grandfather had just had open-heart surgery, and she traveled there to be with him. Her grandparents, Azim's parents, lived fairly close to her other grandparents, also in Vancouver, and the families stayed in contact even after Azim and Almas' divorce. Tasreen and her mother flew to San Diego. When they arrived at the Vancouver airport counter, Tasreen had to support her mother so she could simply remain standing. Tasreen decided she would need to stay strong for her mother.

Tasreen and Tariq Khamisa at Tasreen's college graduation

As they were attempting to make sense of the senseless act, Tasreen felt only anger. She was angry at DiMille's for sending her brother on a pizza run that was dangerous. When Tasreen's parents left to identify Tariq's body, the manager of DiMille's called to check on the family. Tasreen answered the phone, and once she realized who it was, she started yelling at him.

"Why would you send my brother to somewhere that wasn't safe?" she barked into the phone, not really expecting an answer.

100

"Why wouldn't you verify the address? Didn't you know that the address was a fake?!" Her deep pain made her want to be mean to someone to offload some of her own hurt. The angrier she got with the manager, the more he tried to calm her down. The employees at DiMille's thought of Tariq as family, and they were hurting, too, while trying to figure out how to support Tariq's real family.

To Tasreen, it wasn't important that the manager answered her or explained himself. No one knew who had killed Tariq, and with the mountain of grief she was bearing, Tasreen needed to blame someone. For her it was DiMille's.

When she wasn't angry, she went through the motions of the aftermath. A family friend planned the memorial service for a few days after the shooting. The actual funeral would take place in Vancouver because neither of Tasreen's grandparents could travel to San Diego. Before the memorial service, different people from San Diego, many who didn't even know Tariq, left cards and flowers at the site of the shooting. The Shia Ismaili community that Azim was part of came together and took care of everyone in the family. Food kept showing up at Azim's house. The days seemed to blur together for the Khamisas, but their community made sure their daily needs were met.

Tasreen felt as though she were in an all-consuming fog. She had to decide which of her many emotions she would listen to. When she decided to stay strong for her mother and father, she also decided not to give in to any of the extreme emotions she was feeling — neither anger nor sadness. At Tariq's memorial service, Tasreen wrote something to be read by someone else. She didn't trust her voice to stay strong enough to be heard during the service.

"Tariq is the most beautiful person I know. He has such a big heart and he gave everything of himself to his family and friends. He touched everyone he met with his unique free-spirited personality.

101

He was a giving, sincere and very real person. I feel so fortunate and blessed to have been his sister. There are no words to describe the feelings I have for him and the pain I feel for our loss. My life will never be the same again. I will cherish our wonderful memories and always keep you close to my heart. I love you with all my heart and miss you so very much."

Surrounded by family during the whirlwind of memorials, Tasreen didn't give herself a lot of room to grieve. She felt compelled to stay strong for other people around her. Soon after the memorial in San Diego, Tasreen's parents and Jennifer, Tariq's girlfriend, flew to Seattle and then drove together to Vancouver. On this drive they heard Tony Hicks' name for the first time and that he had been arrested. When they found out that Tony was the one responsible for Tariq's shooting, and that he was only 14, Tasreen's anger shifted toward him and away from DiMille's. But she felt conflicted. She had majored in sociology in college, which is the study of social problems and how people interact with others. Her focus was specifically on juvenile delinquency, and she had studied the reasons children act violently. That usually happened when they had been exposed to trauma in their lives, and knowing this made it impossible for Tasreen to throw 100 percent of her anger at Tony. However, the part of her that just felt without letting her brain get in the way was extremely angry at the 14-year-old who killed her brother. Her brother was everything to her, and in some ways it felt like a part of her was also gone. She went back and forth between anger that comes from senseless loss and the empathy that comes from understanding why kids Tony's age commit crimes like this.

When Tasreen returned to Seattle after the funeral, she felt like she was able to get away from the craziness of the situation in San Diego. In San Diego, a media frenzy formed around all the details of the case as Tony was the youngest person ever to be tried as an adult in California. In Seattle, she could hide from the media and focus on staying strong for her mother. Tasreen gave up her apartment and decided to move back into her mother's house — the house where Tasreen and Tariq had lived as teenagers. The days started to bleed into each other as they repeated similar patterns. For the first 40 days, as is expected in the Muslim faith, they went to mosque to help Tariq's soul move on into the next phase. Tasreen's days were mostly identical. She would wake up, go to work, come home and go to the mosque with her mom. For at least the first six months, Tasreen just went through the motions of life. It was as if she were watching the world but wasn't really in it. Her life was joyless, but she felt compelled to stay strong for her mother.

After the memorials were finished and Tasreen settled into her new "normal" life, she mostly stayed in Seattle. A few events brought her to San Diego. Her father was working to start a foundation in her brother's name, and Tasreen visited to stay loosely connected to this work. Sometimes on these visits she would also see Jennifer. On one of these visits, they met at Balboa Park, which stretched for miles through the heart of San Diego. They met under Tariq's favorite tree. When Tasreen was in Seattle, she could choose to think about her brother and experience sadness and anger. Or she could choose not to. In San Diego, she couldn't avoid thinking and talking about her brother. When she met with Jennifer, they always talked about Tariq. Jennifer couldn't believe he was gone, and she was buried in her grief. Even if they didn't meet in person, Tasreen and Jennifer spoke on the phone about Tariq at least once a week. However, after a year of weekly contact, Jennifer decided it was too difficult to be around Tasreen. She told her that Tasreen reminded her too much of Tariq, and it hurt her to be near Tasreen. Although it was difficult

103

Tasreen Khamisa during the early years of TKF, in the office

to hear this at first, Tasreen decided she needed to give Jennifer space, and then eventually she let her go. They intentionally lost contact.

In Seattle, Tasreen was still able to choose not to fully confront her loss. She began going out more with friends to parties or clubs. In college she had been busy working full time and taking a full course load. After college, Tasreen started a temporary job as a receptionist at a print house. When that business closed, one of the clients asked Tasreen to work with her as an advertising assistant at a company that published two magazines. By the time of Tariq's death, she was a head print buyer for the multimillion-dollar company, working full days. This was never a job she planned for, but after Tariq's death, she was able to get lost in the color checks and working with graphic designers and advertisers to make sure everything was perfect before going to print. She could momentarily forget about her brother. Although she didn't love the work, she didn't have to think about her brother's death during the day because her mind was occupied. Outside of work, she kept busy with friends and going out.

One night when Tasreen was out at a club with her cousin and best friend, she met a man named Kalani who quickly became her boyfriend. He was a medic in the Army, and she was drawn to the spiritual side of him. Kalani was also a practicing Buddhist. He brought the fun back into Tasreen's life. When Kalani could leave the Army base, they often went out for dinner or to a karaoke bar. Tasreen would watch and Kalani would sing. His go-to karaoke songs were anything reggae. Together they felt carefree in life yet grounded in spirituality. And then, 18 months after Tariq's death, and six months after Tasreen and Kalani had gotten together, Kalani killed himself after he was dishonorably discharged from the Army.

Again Tasreen found herself confronted with a senseless death, and it was at this point that she hit rock bottom. She realized she couldn't ignore the pain and grief anymore. With the help of her family, she dove right into the pain. Her father decided she needed to get away from everything to really reset and begin to work through her grief. They went on a month long trip to Europe. Her father knew the importance of changing the scene to get a new perspective on life. They went to Scotland to visit family, and they traveled to Paris and the south of France. Her father rented a car, and they traveled around trying new restaurants and doing all the sightseeing they could. It felt like a vacation from her crushing real life.

Boarding the plane to return to the U.S., she felt overwhelmed with the prospect of having to transition back to reality. Tasreen realized she needed help to process her grief. Before Kalani's suicide, she worked hard to keep herself busy by being the supportive daughter and friend, and the dedicated employee. Now she realized this had all been a way to distract herself from the trauma she had experienced over the last 18 months.

Tasreen began seeing a therapist regularly. With the therapist, Tasreen didn't need to worry about protecting anyone else's feelings when talking about her brother. Instead, she could just confront the grief and really start to work through it. And she began volunteering at her mosque, where she became a program officer for some of the youth programming. The work at her mosque felt meaningful, nothing like the work she was doing as a print buyer. Ever since college, she had known she wanted to work with kids.

As Tasreen spent more and more time committed to working with the youth at her mosque, she started to feel like she was climbing out of a deep hole of grief. She realized that as she worked in the service of other people, she thought less about herself. She didn't want to feel like a victim anymore. She was tired of always feeling sad or angry or unable to get out of bed. The combination of therapy and the volunteer work with kids was the spark she needed. Grieving in a healthy way allowed her to finally begin to come to terms with Tariq's death.

Meanwhile, Tasreen's father was doing a different type of work in San Diego. Azim poured himself into the foundation, and two years after their father-daughter trip to Europe, Tasreen moved to San Diego to work for TKF.

She was in awe of her father for starting the foundation when it began in October 1995. By the end of 1996, after Europe but before she was ready to move to San Diego, Tasreen was placed on the board of the foundation. This position was mostly in name only and didn't require her to take much action. Normally a board helps direct the vision of an organization and votes on big decisions. Although she attended a few meetings and events, she wasn't engaged in a deep way. Before moving to San Diego, she kept up with the work of TKF, but through the lens of an outsider.

On her first day really working for TKF, Tasreen had a completely different feeling when she walked through the door. The foundation was located in a small office in downtown San Diego, in a space a supportive law firm let them use at no charge. The foundation was working with at-risk youth and telling the story of Tariq and Tony with the hope of preventing youth violence. The staff numbered two; Tasreen was now one of those two. The first day of work was the hardest. Doing basic administrative tasks, she no longer had the luxury of choosing when she wanted to think about her brother's death. She soon realized she would have to say his name every time she answered the phone.

"Hello. This is the Tariq Khamisa Foundation. Can I help you?"

Just saying Tariq's name made her think about him. The first few months were incredibly difficult and painful. She was living in a new city, leaving her family and friends behind in Seattle. But eventually she started to feel as though she were finally finding her footing and standing on solid ground again. She started to fall in love with work, and this was when Tasreen's healing really started. She realized that she had to know her pain to be able to get to the other side of it.

Working at TKF also forced her to think about Tony. As she worked with Ples and learned more about Tony's story, Tasreen's empathy grew stronger, eventually winning out over her anger. She felt like her empathy muscle was finally lifting her spirits, and it strengthened as she learned about Tony's life leading up to the night of the shooting. Ples was really involved with the staff, and she learned about Tony from him. She started reading through interviews

Tasreen Khamisa with a student

with Tony that a filmmaker had produced. Since TKF was putting together a video to use in its assemblies, she read through all of the material to help with this.

Originally, TKF asked if Tasreen would just work for six months to test it out and see if she liked it. She fell in love with the work and stayed. Tasreen worked over the next six years to grow the foundation to be able to work with as many kids as they could while still honoring her brother. Almost immediately she felt that work at TKF was her path in life. While working, she felt her brother guiding her. She started making decisions and shaping the organization in ways she never thought she could. It required a certain level of confidence that was built from coming out on the other side of her pain

Forgiveness was at the core of Tasreen's journey, but it was shrouded in different layers. Working at the foundation allowed her to peel the first layer and get closer to the core of forgiveness. Through her work at the mosque in Seattle and her efforts at TKF, Tasreen was working for the good of others. This gave her a renewed purpose, and it let the anger start to slide away. However, once the anger and resentment faded away, she was finally able to release the painful feelings she had. Gratefully, she realized all of those emotions were no longer controlling her. There was no guidebook to tell her when she would get closer to the next layer of forgiveness, but she started working toward it once the anger was no longer in her way.

The second layer of forgiveness for Tasreen was finding empathy for Tony and wishing him well. Although her father had met Tony and had been communicating with him, Tasreen wasn't interested in meeting Tony during her journey of forgiveness for many years. Releasing the anger and resentment from her heart allowed her to empathize with Tony's story. Yet, it didn't make her ready to meet him face to face.

Tasreen settled into San Diego, where she met a man she fell in love with and eventually married. They met through a childhood friend when Tasreen wasn't looking to start a relationship.

As TKF continued to grow over the next six years, Tasreen decided she would leave the foundation to start a family. The foundation felt stable. It had grown from a staff of two to a staff of seven. Funding to run the programs was also stable. A five-year strategic plan was in place, and they had hired a development director. The foundation was working with middle schools in San Diego to give students the tools to navigate life and their emotions in a healthy way. TKF offered three programs to middle schools, and they were reaching thousands of kids a year. These programs showed students that they didn't have to walk their journeys alone. The hope was that students would be able to ground themselves in who they were so they wouldn't need to look externally for someone or something to validate them. After leaving her job at TKF, she remained on the board and remained connected to the work. Her forgiveness journey toward Tony had reached a plateau. She held no ill will for Tony. To her, TKF was all about her brother, and she was able to still remain mostly detached from forging a connection with Tony while honoring the memory of her brother. Tony was a person she had named when she told and retold her brother's story, but even saying his name out loud evoked only neutral feelings toward the victim at the other end of the gun.

Although Tasreen had grown to love and respect Ples, she did not feel ready to forge a similar relationship with his grandson. However, at the beginning of 2014, after 11 years, Tasreen decided to come back to the foundation, and something felt different. Her marriage had dissolved and ended in a divorce. She realized that she needed to do the hard inner work to help her heal from her relationship.

As she explored areas in her life that she wanted to address and heal from, her thoughts turned to Tony. Enough time had passed that she felt like she was ready to finally meet Tony face to face. Putting this feeling into words was difficult. However, she felt ready to peel back another layer toward forgiveness. Perhaps it was all wrapped up in healing all areas of her life. There was a push in TKF to heal the perpetrator, and she realized she needed to be a part of that for Tony. It was a strong feeling, and it felt right that she should reach out and meet Tony now that she was back and immersed in the work of the foundation.

This was a huge and heavy layer to peel off on her forgiveness journey. She wanted to meet the boy, who was now a man, who had taken her brother's life. Once she decided to meet him, they wrote letters to each other at first. Eventually, her visitation form was approved. The night before the meeting, Tasreen couldn't sleep. She lay in bed wondering: *How am I going to really feel about this person when I look him in the eyes?* Ples had agreed to accompany Tasreen, and being with Ples made her feel comfortable.

They made arrangements to travel to Centinela State Prison in Imperial County, California. Tasreen drove to Ples' house first, and then he drove them to the prison. The car ride with Ples was very quiet. Tasreen was nervous and her stomach felt unsettled. Ples could tell that she needed to sit in her space quietly so he didn't push her to speak on the ride.

When they entered the visitation room, Tasreen and Ples sat down before they called Tony to meet them. The room was big, but it felt cold. Rows of vending machines lined one wall. The round tables were built low to the ground so inmates could keep their hands on the table and visible at all times. The guards sat at higher tables so they could scan the room easily. When inmates were brought in, they were made to sit so their backs were never to the guards. Tasreen knew ahead of time that inmates were only allowed to hug hello and goodbye. Tony walked in and hugged Ples before greeting Tasreen. There was a slight hesitation at first, but she had felt comfortable from seeing his greeting with Ples. Tasreen and Tony hugged hello. His hug was strong but warm. She felt safe immediately. It felt like her brother's energy was surrounding them.

"Wow, you're really short," Tony said when he finally spoke.

"You're really tall," Tasreen responded.

Tony and Tasreen immediately fell into a playful back-and-forth. It felt so similar to the laughter and the teasing that had been a big part of her relationship with Tariq. The playfulness lifted the seriousness of the meeting. Right away, Tasreen's connection to Tony

111

The day Tasreen Khamisa met Tony Hicks for the first time, accompanied by Ples Felix

felt comfortable and light. She thought to herself, *This is a really cool guy.*

Tony had been in prison for 20 years before he and Tasreen developed their friendship. Tasreen recognized that the final layer of forgiveness is peeled away when two people come together to make something more positive. They began to talk every week. Inmates had to schedule their phone calls, which were limited to 15 minutes. Tony arranged to call Tasreen every weekend. Tasreen looked forward to these calls, and she knew there would be a lot of laughter and support for each other in these conversations.

A few years into their friendship, they spoke about Jennifer. Through reflection, Tony realized that he took two lives the night Tariq was killed. He felt responsible for Jennifer's suicide. Tony thought about this as he began planning for his first meeting with the parole board. Processing all of this with Tasreen proved powerful and almost unbelievable in many ways. As part of his preparation for the hearing, Tony was required to make a list of people he would be able to count on if he were to be released. This would be his circle of support.

One day on the phone, Tony asked Tasreen, "Could you be in my circle of support?"

"Of course," she said, "I'm already in your circle of support!"

As part of his circle, Tasreen wanted to make sure Tony never returned to prison. In the United States, California has one of the highest rates of recidivism—when someone commits a crime again after being released from prison. The relationship that Tasreen and Tony built has become that of siblings, and she can't lose a brother again.

As Tasreen waits for the parole hearing, she preps with Tony and hopes that one day they will work side by side at the foundation. She is surrounded by optimism — from her father, from Ples, her mother and the entire network of TKF. Most of all, she is inspired by Tony's growth. Although she knows it takes time to forgive and each person's path is different, it was the best thing she could have done for herself. By arriving at a place of forgiveness, a whole new world has opened up for Tasreen. She is surrounded by her brother's energy and lightness in her friendship with Tony, who has grown lifetimes older than the 14-year-old boy who made a terrible choice on one single night of his life.

Part Five

Closing: Tony's Letter to Tariq

While in prison, Tony began answering questions from students who were involved in the Tariq Khamisa Foundation programming. He replied in hand-written letters he mailed to TKF. In 2018, he received the question below, which he answered in the form of a letter to Tariq.

Question: What if you had one chance to talk to Tariq. What would you say?

Tariq,

There are no words to express how sorry I am for taking your life and putting your family through so much pain. I bear the responsibility for what happened that night on January 21, 1995, not just for murdering you but for the role I played leading up to my attempting to rob you and ultimately shooting and killing you. I could have prevented this senseless tragedy in a number of ways: by speaking out against it when the idea was first introduced in that small apartment to rob a pizza man or refusing to return to the apartment with the bogus address that you would be sent to. I could have said no to the gun that was handed to me as I watched you from across the street unable to find an address that I knew didn't exist. But I did none of these because my need to be accepted by my peers meant more to me, at that time, than your well-being or your life.

It's sad as I look back on it, how I fought to hide my insecurities from the world instead of speaking to someone about them, getting help for them. I filtered my life through those insecurities and made decisions based on the distorted perception they provided me, and one of those decisions ended your life, shattered the lives of all those that loved you and traumatized the community.

I can't comprehend what you must have felt that night I ambushed you, turning around to see me standing there with a loaded gun pointing at you demanding the pizza that you had already returned to the back of the car. You were courageous in that moment refusing to allow yourself to be robbed and for standing for what was right.

I often wonder if I would have your strength now? I know that I didn't have it then. I was scared and weak inside trying to hide those feelings and others behind the mask that being a part of a gang provided me and the gun that I pointed at you. I wish I had been stronger then. Instead I acted out of my cowardness when I murdered you. I robbed you of the life you should have had, the love that you shared, the unlimited potential that you possess and I am extremely sorry for that. I don't want to insult you by saying that I have the capacity to fully understand the impact on your family that your murder has had. I know that it has sent a ripple effect of confusion, pain and loss through their lives and it shames me now to know that I am responsible for not just your murder but the effect that your murder has had on so many others.

Your father Azim forgave me for killing you after I was arrested. He even came to visit me in prison 3 years after your death. The compassion that he has shown me is humbling. I also communicate with Tasreen often, she has opened her life up to me and I feel so blessed to know her. Through them I have learned more about you and through you than I've learned about myself.

You may not know this but I've begun to appreciate how your death has impacted so many young lives in a positive way. Through the foundation, named in your honor, Azim and my grandfather share our story to countless numbers of people providing a message of empathy, nonviolence, and forgiveness which continues to resonate for so many even after all these years.

I greatly admire the work that they are doing with the foundation. It is an honor for me to be able to be a part of the good work that is being done in your name. I know that I can never do enough to make right what I've done. Murdering you was a decision I would take back if I could, I would give you back to your family if I had that power. I am striving, every day, to be a better person than I was yesterday. Over the years I've resolved the insecurities that I filtered my life through. I hope to be of service to others in a positive way now. I will spend my life making amends for taking your life and those I have hurt along this journey, I will do it all in your name Tariq.

— Tony Hicks, April 9, 2018

The Story of This Book:

Acknowledgements

The first time I heard of the Tariq Khamisa Foundation, I was struck by the powerful story. I was conducting a site visit for one of my high school students who was interning in the office with the TKF staff. As I walked to my car after leaving the building, I carried with me the powerful story Tasreen had shared, which only scratched the surface of why TKF was doing work in schools. Forgiveness seemed like such an impossible action after Tasreen's brother had been killed. Yet, she told the story to me with the calm tone of someone who has truly healed and feels fulfilled in her work. When she shared the work that she had been doing on behalf of TKF to ensure that Tony Hicks would receive parole, I knew that I wanted to help share the story with a wider reach. A lot of their work had been local to San Diego and Southern California, and I wondered how this inspirational story could be spread. As an educator, I knew how powerful the message of forgiveness could be. I also knew first-hand that students have to make difficult choices every day. I joined with another teacher, Corey Clark, and his seventh graders to create and publish this writing.

For me, writing has always been a collaborative process. This book started with interviews of the Khamisa family, Ples Felix and Tony Hicks. Everyone was extremely generous with their time and emotions. Telling and retelling the story of Tariq's life and death brings feelings to the surface for everyone involved. And we resurfaced sadness, excitement, anger, exhaustion, confusion, healing and joy. Through interviews, documents and photos, I pieced together a first draft of each of these sections. However, I knew that the story would connect with students on a deeper level if the seventh graders in Mr. Clark's class helped me tell it. They spent time in class and out of class as my editors. They asked questions and gave feedback on each section, making sure we had enough details to tell the story while also honoring each person's journey on this Earth. They met with me during their lunchtimes, during class and after school. These seventh graders also interviewed Ples Felix and members of the Khamisa family. They wrote letters to Tony while he was in prison. And they suggested that they add a preface that could start with the synopsis to pull the readers in. This process allowed the writing to emerge in a truly collaborative way.

Many voices come out clearly in this story, but we know that each reader will connect with the story in different ways. You all will have heard these voices differently, and the story may have brought up different emotions based on your own personal background. Our hope for this work is that everyone reading this story will use it as an inspiration to make nonviolent choices in your lives.

I would like to leave you with words written by Tariq Khamisa when he was a high school student. It was part of his Philosophy of Life that he developed for a school assignment: "I feel time is the

120

most precious commodity known to man; because once it's gone, it's gone forever. Time is one thing you can never get back ... so you should always spend your time wisely."

I hope that you will choose to spend your time as peacemakers in your schools and communities. Thank you for reading this story.

Tony Hicks granted parole and released from prison

Tony Hicks answering questions from students
at a TKF Peacemaker Assembly

Tony Hicks and Azim Khamisa hang out
for the first time after Tony's release
from prison

Tony Hicks and Ples Felix on Father's Day

Tony Hicks and Tasreen Khamisa outside of the TKF office

Ples Felix, Tony Hicks, and Azim Khamisa

Ples Felix, Tony Hicks, Azim Khamisa, and Tasreen Khamisa

Made in the USA
Middletown, DE
01 May 2022

64952361R00080